Praise for *Every Reason to Leave*

Vicki Rose is a trophy of God's grace, as is her marriage to Bill Rose. Her story is a powerful testimony of God's ability to redeem the most hopeless situation. In a day when so many marriages are not making it to the finish line, this is a story that needs to be heard. I believe Vicki's life message will be a healing balm to many women in difficult marriages and will give them the courage and faith to wait on the Lord and remain faithful to Him and His calling, rather than throwing in the towel on their marriage. Above all, I trust it will stir up in every wife a desire for her marriage to better reflect the amazing redemptive story of Christ and His bride.

> —**Nancy Leigh DeMoss**, author, host of *Revive Our Hearts* radio

I have never read a more compelling account of the power of God to change lives and restore marriages. In her book *Every Reason to Leave*, Vicki Rose shares her journey with integrity—the good, the bad, the horrible, the separation, the discovery, the restoration, the work, and the deep satisfaction. Walking this road with Billy and Vicki has the potential of changing your life forever. I wish every couple—married or divorced—could read this book.

> —**Gary Chapman** PhD, bestselling author of *The 5 Love Languages*

Searching for happiness and wholeness, Vicki Rose chased after those high society offerings she envisioned would bring her significance and satisfaction. However, in chasing her dreams, her life turned more and more into a nightmare. Her story describes setbacks and disappointments, especially in her early years of marriage to Billy Rose, partial owner of the New York Yankees. As I read this book, I could not put it down. Trust me, you have every reason to read *Every Reason to Leave*, especially if you are in a crisis in your marriage and/or in your faith. Don't leave either, and Vicki will give you the reason.

> —**Emerson Eggerichs** PhD, author of *Love and Respect*

Staying married, growing old together, loving and caring for each other as we age and decline—this is but one area Vicki Rose touches on in *Every Reason to Leave*. The joy of a thirty-seven-plus-year marriage relationship that has persevered through drug addiction, infidelity, and five years of separation to victory through a relationship with Jesus Christ is the subject of this testimonial work. This is a must-read for anyone contemplating divorce!

> —**Don P. Hodel**, former president and CEO of Focus on the Family

D1310192

Every Reason to Leave is not for the fainthearted. It took enormous courage and patience for Vicki Rose to say no to divorce and yes to waiting for the Lord to heal her wounded heart and her marriage. With devastating insight into how it takes two sinners to kill a marriage, but only one Savior to restore it, Vicki crafts an insightful account that will be both a beacon and a road map to the countless couples who live in quiet desperation.

—**Barbara Ryan,** attorney, speaker, pastoral caregiver

Marriage is tricky business, and how you handle the trickiness might just make or break the rest of your life. My friends Bill and Vicki have navigated their way through the challenges, proving that anyone who surrenders to the will and ways of Jesus can enjoy the mutual intimacy of a deep and abiding love. I have watched their relationship . . . it is the real deal. Thanks, Bill and Vicki, for this compelling story! Many will find hope in their journey toward a fulfilling marriage because you have shared your struggles and victories with such transparency and power.

—**Dr. Joseph M. Stowell,** president, Cornerstone University

This book is the blood, sweat, and tears of a woman who had the courage to stay married when her marriage was not a fairy tale. Vicki writes about principles that she has not only learned but also has lived. Her story is a miracle that will challenge and offer hope to any twenty-first-century wife who would consider staying married in the midst of difficult, shattering, non-fairy tale circumstances.

—**Jackie Kendall,** president of Power to Grow and bestselling
author of *Lady in Waiting*

Like Vicki and Billy, we found our marriage in trouble and had serious doubts about our future together. If we'd had the chance to read this honest and provocative book back then, we might have better understood God's plan for vibrant relationships and avoided some hard lessons. Reading Vicki and Billy's story and the transformation that God brought about because this couple chose to honor their marriage vows will be of great encouragement to women who have all but given up on their marriages. This book is a must-read for the discouraged and disheartened!

—**Norm and Bobbe Evans,** founders, The Winning Ways

For those who feel they have no hope, this book is for you. If life feels meaningless or is imploding, you will find solace and comfort in this gripping story of a NYC Jewish socialite couple who found a radical means of healing. For singles or the average couple, you will learn capacities for new depths of forgiveness toward all your friends and family. I had a front row seat for this modern-day miracle. Do yourself a favor—grab this book!

—**Sheila Weber,** executive director, National Marriage Week USA

EVERY REASON
TO LEAVE

& why we chose to stay together

VICKI ROSE

WITH DANA WILKERSON

MOODY PUBLISHERS

CHICAGO

All Scripture quotations, unless otherwise indicated, are taken from the *The Holy Bible, English Standard Version.* Copyright © 2000, 2001 by Crossway Bibles. a division of Good News Publishers. Used by permission. All rights reserved.

Scripture quotations marked NLT are from *The Holy Bible, New Living Translation,* copyright © 1996, 2004. Used by permission of Tyndale House Publishers, Inc., Wheaton, IL, 60189, U.S.A. All rights reserved.

Scripture quotations marked NIV are taken from the *Holy Bible, New International Version®*, NIV®. Copyright ©1973, 1978, 1984 by Biblica, Inc.™ Used by permission of Zondervan. All rights reserved worldwide. www.zondervan.com. The "NIV" and "New International Version" are trademarks registered in the United States Patent and Trademark Office by Biblica, Inc.™

All emphases in Scripture quotations have been added by the author.

Edited by Lydia Brownback
Interior design: Ragont Design
Cover design: Faceout Studio, Tim Green
Cover images: Getty #135964555 / Shutterstock #169749833
Author photo: Jeff Calenberg

Library of Congress Cataloging-in-Publication Data
Rose, Vicki.
  Every reason to leave : and why we chose to stay together / by Vicki Rose, with Dana Wilkerson.
    pages cm
  Includes bibliographical references.
  ISBN 978-0-8024-0655-2
  1. Marriage—Religious aspects—Christianity. 2. Divorce—Religious aspects—Christianity. I. Title.
  BV835.R674 2014
  248.8'44—dc23
                          2014008835

We hope you enjoy this book from Moody Publishers. Our goal is to provide high-quality, thought-provoking books and products that connect truth to your real needs and challenges. For more information on other books and products written and produced from a biblical perspective, go to www.moodypublishers.com or write to:

Moody Publishers
820 N. LaSalle Boulevard
Chicago, IL 60610

1a 3 5 7 9 10 8 6 4 2

Printed in the United States of America

To Billy
For your perseverance in our marriage
For your love for God
For loving me forever and always
For becoming my best friend
And for loving our children and grands
You make my black and white life an adventure in living color
I love you forever!

CONTENTS

INTRODUCTION

THIS BOOK IS WRITTEN FOR THOSE who are wondering if
staying married is worth the effort. It is written for those who think
a different husband or wife is the answer to their problems. It is for
those who have "fallen out of love" and who think that "being in love"
is the answer. It is for those who are bored by their husband or wife and
those who think their spouse is not good enough or successful enough.
It is for those whose spouse has been unfaithful, cares more about work
than family, or puts the kids before all else. It is for spouses who have
many interests in common and for those who are totally different. It is
for those who want more spice in their lives and for those who want
more calm.

Basically, if you are anywhere from struggling to acutely miserable
in your marriage and want to call it quits, this book is for you. My husband and I were separated for five and a half years. During that time,
our lives were transformed through a relationship with God. We then
sought counseling and have seen our marriage repaired, healed, and
changed into a relationship about which I had only dared to dream. It
has taken time, commitment, and lots of very hard work. It has taken
friends believing in us and coming alongside of us. It has taken prayer,
patience, giving up of some of our desires, and much, much more.

In his book *Sacred Marriage*, Gary Thomas asks the question,
"What if God designed marriage to make us holy more than to make
us happy?"[1] God does not promise happiness or an easy life or marriage. Our culture fools us into thinking that happiness is a goal of
life. I know from my own experience that living for happiness is a lie.

The more I sought happiness in my life, the more miserable I became. Instead, I found the answer to life in God Himself and His Word: "But seek first his kingdom and his righteousness, and all these things will be given to you as well" (Matt. 6:33).

God has brought my husband and me to a great place of victory in our marriage over the past two decades. I want to share our journey with you so that you might be encouraged in yours—encouraged to ask and seek God for restoration and victory for whatever you are facing in your marriage, separation, or even divorce. I want to cheer you on to prevent the regret that comes from walking away from something God can heal.

We have discovered the joy that being married for the long term brings. Through all sorts of trials and hardships and living life together, we know the joy of lifelong love. In our fight for our marriage, we have both been changed into someone the other respects. We have also seen the regret of others who have quit their marriage, only to exchange their present issues for a whole new set of problems.

It is my hope that God will use this book—our story—to give you the desire, the courage, and the commitment necessary to stay in your marriage and to know that you are not alone!

Chapter 1

IN THE BEGINNING

WHEN MY HUSBAND AND I do speaking engagements together, we like to do this little routine:

Vicki: I like to get up early, around 5:30 or 6:00. I love the morning.

Billy: I hate early.

Vicki: I like ballet, and I love the theater.

Billy: I could watch ESPN all day and be perfectly happy.

Vicki: I like the house quiet. If it were up to me, we would not have a TV.

Billy: With nine TVs in our new apartment, a pitch, a pass, a putt, or a punt is not missed.

Vicki: I know that traffic lights are given by God to bring order to my life.

Billy: In New York City, traffic lights are a suggestion only, and I believe they're a tool of Satan to disrupt my whole day's plans.

Vicki: I love to plan in advance.

Billy: I don't understand that. Why would you want to plan in advance when you know the best offer is going to come along at the last minute?

Vicki: At the end of the day I really like to talk about everything we've gone through, every situation we've faced.

Billy: Why do women find it necessary to talk about the stuff that
         you just lived through all day? It makes absolutely no sense
         at all.

Billy and I are opposites in so many ways that you might wonder
how we ever ended up together and are still married nearly forty years
after taking our vows. Throughout this book you'll get to read a lot
about how we've managed to stay married. But in order to fully understand our story, it's important that you know where we came from and
how we ended up together.

YOUNG BILLY ROSE

William Stuart Rose was born on July 2, 1952, and grew up in
a Jewish family in Manhattan. However, Judaism was never a big
factor in Billy's childhood. In fact, he went to Trinity School—a private school in New York City—where he attended Christian chapel
every day. Billy remembers going to temple as a child only on some of
the High Holy Days. The problem was, the High Holy Days occurred
during the World Series (which took place in September back then).
His mom wouldn't let him miss school to watch his beloved Yankees
play in the World Series unless he went to temple first. So to temple he
went and then headed off to baseball's temple: Yankee Stadium. Billy
remembers watching Mickey Mantle hit a home run to win that game,
though the Yankees ended up losing the series.

Billy had a terrific childhood. His parents were his two closest
friends and were very dear to his heart. His dad was fifty-six when
Billy was born, and he was twenty-five years older than Billy's mom.
Nevertheless, Billy and his dad would play ball together all the time—
Wiffle ball, that is. They would play in the hallway of their New York
City apartment, with Billy's mom yelling at them as antiques crashed
to the floor.

Billy dreamed of playing professional baseball, so he worked hard at his game. He taught himself to bat left-handed, and he consistently hit over .400 after he became a switch-hitter. After his sophomore year of high school, he transferred to a prep school in Connecticut, where he was captain of the baseball team. During his junior year he had verbal offers from two major league teams—the Cleveland Indians and the Boston Red Sox. He was disappointed that the Yankees weren't showing interest, but any interest was good. Both teams told him if he played as well during his senior year as he had during his junior year, they would come back and sign him. Billy was also offered a full scholarship to play baseball at Arizona State University. Unfortunately, during his senior year of high school, Billy had a career-ending knee injury and was never able to play either college or professional baseball.

Since collegiate baseball was no longer an option, Billy headed off to Franklin and Marshall College in Lancaster, Pennsylvania. Never one to do much in the way of academics, Billy likes to joke, "College would have been perfect if it weren't for the classes." He changed majors three times before he found one he liked that didn't include any math. He finally settled on political science. Billy and two friends pledged a fraternity, but after their rush experience, they decided to depledge. They convinced their parents to rent them an apartment, which is common now but wasn't in the early seventies. Their apartment became party central, and they practically put the fraternities out of business. Billy graduated in 1974, but he didn't even stick around for the commencement ceremony. His parents weren't thrilled, but he didn't want to go back just for graduation.

Not too long after college, Billy was introduced to George Steinbrenner—then the principal owner and managing partner of the Yankees—through a mutual friend. George presented Billy with two job offers. He could manage the Yankees Class-A minor league baseball team in Fort Lauderdale or take the position of general manager of the Yankees AAA minor league team in Syracuse. He turned them both down, because although he loved baseball and the Yankees, he wasn't sure he could work for George. He was much happier being his friend.

Part of the reason Billy was easily able to turn down Mr. Steinbrenner's offers was that he had a job in the family business, Fabrics by William Rose, a premiere textile company that supplied fabric to Seventh Avenue's top dress and sportswear designers. They imported fabric from Europe and sold it to higher-priced dress designers such as Anne Klein, Calvin Klein, and Oscar de la Renta. However, Billy did become involved in the baseball business in 1976 when he and his dad purchased a minority stake in the Yankees, which we still hold today.

MY TURBULENT CHILDHOOD

I, Victoria Ellen Gage, was born on January 3, 1953, also to Jewish parents in Manhattan. My father was a hardworking stockbroker with little patience for those who didn't work hard. My mother was a full-time, stay-at-home mom as well as a perfectionist with an unpredictable temper. Both of my parents were highly critical.

My older sister, Heidi, and I are four years apart, and though we are the best of friends now and extremely close, we fought bitterly when we were growing up. I was jealous of her beauty, her boyfriends, and her abilities, and I spent a good part of my childhood and early adulthood trying to outdo her in any way I could. We both attended the Spence School, a private school for girls in New York City. There I was known as "Heidi's little sister" and was often called by her name, which I hated. I felt like I was invisible. That experience put in me a desire to be noticed.

When I was ten, my Jewish family joined a Presbyterian church for both social and religious reasons, none of which I understood. I memorized the Twenty-third Psalm and the Apostles' Creed. I went to Sunday school and confirmation class. I was even on a radio Bible quiz show as part of Sunday school one morning. But I did not know God; I didn't have a personal relationship with Him at the time or even know what that was. I knew *about* God. I believed that He was up there in the sky someplace and that I was down here on earth, but that was about all we had to do with each other. As a result, there was a lot of emptiness in my heart.

All kids have a dream, and I was no exception. But instead of dreaming of becoming a teacher or a nurse or a lawyer or a mother, I dreamed of being noticed, of being rich and famous. I would come home from school each day, and there on the front-hall table was the retail paper *Women's Wear Daily*. I wasn't interested in the retail part; I turned straight to the society pages. As I read those pages and checked out the glamorous people in the photos each day, I became familiar with the names and faces therein. I knew what they did, what parties they went to, what they wore, and who they hung out with. I started to desire to be one of them. I wanted to be famous. I wanted my life to be significant, and that's what I thought significance was. I bought into the belief that if you have enough money and are noticed enough, then you're happy. And even then I believed that if I couldn't provide that for myself, if I married someone who could provide it, then I would be happy.

I knew that in order to be one of those women, I needed to dress like them. But that was a problem. My mother was constantly critical of my weight and would often ground me when my weight was too high for her liking. She would also tell me I couldn't have any new clothes unless my weight was below a certain amount. This was very distressing to me, as I was not overweight. I was five feet tall and never weighed more than 115 pounds. However, Mom wanted me to be less than 102. So when I was visiting a dermatologist for a skin issue, I casually asked if he could prescribe diet pills, which he did. What I didn't realize was that the pills were habit-forming and highly addictive. I was soon hooked to the point that I needed a pill in order to function properly. But the pills did the work that they were marketed to do, and I was easily able to stay under Mom's weight limit and therefore able to buy new clothes.

As a teenager, I often felt that I didn't measure up to other teens, which was a side effect of my mother's critical spirit. I was embarrassed

about how I looked and therefore felt like an outcast. I was uncomfortable around boys and didn't know how to be a good friend. I was constantly trying to fit with the "in" crowd, but I never felt that I was quite
good enough for them. Many of them came from extremely wealthy
families, and my parents encouraged me to be friendly with them because wealthy people were better than nonwealthy people, so they said.
Since we didn't have as much money as many of my classmates, I took
my parents' words to mean that I wasn't as good as the others were.
This, along with my obsession with *Women's Wear Daily*, caused me to
believe even more strongly that being wealthy and having material pos-
sessions such as fashionable clothes and beautifully decorated homes
was the answer to happiness.

When I was a junior in high school, my mother was diagnosed
with an inoperable type of stomach cancer. Medical and privacy laws
were different then than they are today, and somehow my father was
able to keep Mom, as well as Heidi and me, from finding out about the
diagnosis. He wanted Mom to enjoy what time she had left without
being consumed with worry and fear. After a few months Dad did tell
Heidi and me, but he made us promise not to tell Mom. He wanted us
to know so we'd be on our best behavior for the last months of Mom's
life.

My mom died eight months later, the week before my high school
graduation. Upon her death, my first reaction was fear, but I also felt
liberated because she had been so critical, strict, and overbearing.
When my dad handed Heidi and me a Valium on the morning of the
funeral and said, "Don't cry at the funeral—let's show everyone how
strong we are," I didn't have much trouble following his command. In
fact, during the funeral I felt fairly disconnected and even relieved, as
horrible as that may sound. Mom's illness had been all-consuming, and
her temper had been terrifying. I figured it wouldn't be so bad to live
without her. Even though my world had been turned upside down, I
decided to follow the family pattern of pretending everything was fine,
even when it wasn't.

That summer between high school and college was a whirlwind. Dad, Heidi, and I were busy all the time, but the fact that the three of us spent all summer together illustrates that we weren't as strong as we appeared. We normally didn't hang out with each other, but that summer we invited friends over nearly every night unless someone invited us out. We went to our country home every weekend and often took friends along. Dad even started seeing other women. We drank and partied all summer so we wouldn't have to think about what was missing.

That fall I headed off to Pine Manor Junior College. I loved my time there, and my most glorious memory was performing in a dance role in *Brigadoon*. All the people came and told me how wonderful I had been. It felt really good to be noticed like that, and the attention started to fill the empty place that was growing inside me. While there, I met my long-term boyfriend Bruce.

I transferred to Sarah Lawrence College for my final two years. Bruce and I lived together during much of that time. As an unbeliever, I didn't see anything wrong with that arrangement. And, after all, it was the early seventies. Women were liberated! We could live with whomever we wanted!

In the meantime, Dad remarried, and Bobbie, who had three children, became my stepmother. The apartment where I had grown up was too small for everyone, so Dad moved the new family to a different apartment in Manhattan, which just happened to be in the same building where Billy Rose's family lived.

You may now kiss the bride!
I am officially Mrs. Billy Rose!

Cutting the cake as
Mr. and Mrs. Billy Rose
on February 4, 1977.

Chapter 2

I, VICKI, TAKE THEE, BILLY

WHEN I FINISHED COLLEGE, I WENT to work at Saks Fifth Avenue. I landed a job with their executive training program, hopped on the fast track, and became a buyer in two years. I thought I was really terrific. I believed that working hard and having people recognize me were making a difference in my life, just like I had dreamed as a child. I felt that people respected me for what I had accomplished, and I wanted to keep it that way. I knew if I came across as important and successful, people wouldn't see how insecure I really was inside.

As I had done for much of my life, I outwardly pretended that all was well in Vicki's world. Deep down, I knew I wasn't satisfied and that there had to be more to life than what I was experiencing. However, I didn't know exactly what was missing. And I was not about to admit to anyone not only that I didn't have it but also, frankly, that I didn't know what "it" was. So I pushed down that feeling and continued down the path I was on. I kept trying to find my purpose and fulfillment through my work and through relationships, even though they continually fell short.

A DREAM COME TRUE

A few months after my dad and stepmother had moved into their new apartment, my aunt called and said there was a "nice fellow," Bill Rose, who lived in our building and had seen me and wanted to meet me. I recognized his name because I had seen his sister's picture in the pages of *Women's Wear Daily*. However, I was still dating Bruce at the time, so dating Billy wasn't an option. Several months later, after I had graduated from Sarah Lawrence College and moved back to New York City and was working at Saks, Bruce and I broke up. Soon after that, in November of 1975, I called my aunt to see if that "nice fellow" in my building was still single and interested. He was.

Billy called me and asked if I'd like to go on a date that Saturday night. I was so excited that I immediately accepted instead of trying to play it cool. However, as soon as I hung up the phone, I realized I was scheduled for minor foot surgery that Saturday evening and wouldn't be able to go on the date. I called Billy back to explain the situation. I could tell he was skeptical; how many foot surgeries really happen on a Saturday evening, after all? He probably thought I was just giving him the "I have to wash my hair that night" excuse.

Questionable excuse or not, Billy agreed to call me again the following week. I later found out that he tipped each of our building's doormen ten dollars to watch and see if I came in with a cast on my foot Saturday night. You really can't blame him, can you? It was roughly the equivalent of today's generation checking up on people's excuses, whereabouts, and life events (or daily events) via social media. The doormen reported back to Billy that I did, indeed, come in with a foot cast, which put his mind at ease about my story. I was out of work for a week after the surgery, and Billy called several times to check up on me. I liked talking to him and was pleased that he seemed very kind and concerned about me.

Two weeks later we finally went on our first date. Billy took me to Le Club, an exclusive dinner and dancing establishment known for its upper-crust clientele. Though I could barely dance due to my recent surgery, we had a really nice time. The next morning I woke up wanting to call Billy and invite him over for breakfast. I decided to play it cool, though, and wait for him to call again, which he soon did. Our second date was to a New York Rangers hockey game—a first for me—and afterward we went to dinner at the 21 Club, one of New York's most expensive and elite restaurants. Since my college boyfriend had been a "starving artist," and I had taken on housecleaning jobs so we would have money for dates, I was over the moon about my dates with Billy. They were an awesome and exciting contrast to my previous dating experiences.

Billy gave me a small, diamond heart pendant for Christmas that year, and I thought, *This is the one*. Billy was the man who could provide me with all the things that would make me happy. He had money, he had connections, and he always had plans to do something and go somewhere glamorous. I loved that about him, and I loved that it meant *I* had something to do and somewhere fabulous to go. He represented that lifestyle I had longed for since my early days of poring over *Women's Wear Daily*. If my teenage self could have seen me a decade later, she wouldn't have believed the life I was living.

As you know, Billy loves sports—especially baseball. I did not grow up in a sports family, and I had never been to a baseball game in my life. When we first dated, I went to seventy New York Yankees home games. No, that's not a typo; we went to *seventy* games! It wasn't what I had ever expected I would someday do (I wouldn't have expected to go to even seven Yankees games in my entire lifetime), but it brought me what I had always dreamed of. Sitting in the owner's box, meeting many famous people in that arena, and having a special permit to park in the players' lot at Yankee Stadium all seemed to be what I had been looking for. Completing my desire, *Women's Wear Daily* printed a photo of me clapping and cheering at a Yankees game. I had arrived. My childhood dream had come true.

What didn't occur to me at the time was that I had developed an unhealthy dependence on and attachment to Billy. I was catering to all of his wishes and dreams and interests, and he didn't want to pursue any of my dreams or interests—not that we would have had time. When you go to seventy baseball games in a six-month span, that doesn't leave much time to do anything else. Even though I loved the ballet and the theater, I stopped going because Billy wasn't interested. I would adapt to any situation, even if it meant giving up most of my dreams and desires. After all, my biggest dream and desire was to be "somebody," and I felt I was really somebody when I was with Billy Rose, even though that somebody looked very little like the Vicki Gage of years past. I abandoned who I was—with my strong, controlling, type-A personality—and allowed Billy's equally controlling, type-A personality to overshadow me in the hopes that in the process I could find what I was missing in my life. I also abandoned my friends during that time in favor of the lifestyle Billy was introducing me to. My old friends weren't a part of that world, so I left them behind. Unsurprisingly, I would come to regret that choice, but at the time, I was in pursuit of something bigger and better than my friends could offer me.

Early in 1976, Billy and I moved in together. We were together all the time when we weren't at work anyway, so it only made sense to live together. We also had no qualms about sleeping together. We had both lost our virginity many years before, and sex was just a normal part of dating.

In August of that year, we were dressing to go to a Yankees-Red Sox game. Billy handed me a small box and told me to open it. When I did, a gorgeous sapphire-and-diamond engagement ring winked up at me. I had flashed my left ring finger at Billy frequently during the prior months in an attempt to prod him along to propose. The moment had arrived. "Will you marry me?" Billy asked. I immediately said yes and then called my dad, stepmom, and sister to tell them the great news. Then we headed off to the baseball game, as we had many times before. But this time was different; I was now officially the future Mrs. Billy Rose.

A ROSE-COLORED WEDDING

Just after our engagement, Billy's parents took us to Venice, Italy, for two weeks. It was one of several luxurious trips we would experience with them. While we were there, the four of us discussed wedding plans. I had always dreamed of being married in my beautiful childhood church with its stained-glass windows, magnificent organ, and beautiful velvet-cushioned, wooden pews. I could just imagine myself walking down that aisle. It would be like a fairy-tale wedding, complete with my own prince.

Billy's parents had other plans. "Everyone knows you're Jewish!" they said. Maybe "everyone" did, but I sure didn't. While my parents came from Jewish families, we had never practiced the Jewish faith; we had gone to church! But Billy's parents were adamant, even though they were in no way devout, practicing Jews. They said it would be ridiculous for two Jewish kids to be married in a church. All of their friends would think it was a farce. So since I had no real faith of my own and didn't want to rock the boat with Billy's parents or cause him to change his mind about marrying me, I continued to cater to Billy's wishes and gave up my church wedding dream. Instead, we agreed to hold the wedding and reception in my father's apartment.

Because I had lost my mother, Billy's mom filled that void for me in many ways even though she was very different from my mom. She would take me out to lunch on a regular basis, she called me every day, and she was very attentive. She also took me wedding-dress shopping. I had always imagined myself in a traditional gown with a long train. That would have been fitting for the church wedding I had dreamed about, but that type of dress didn't seem to fit an apartment wedding.

When I arrived at the designer's showroom with my future mother-in-law, I quickly realized the people there were not wedding-dress designers. However, since this was my future mother-in-law's choice of designers, I knew I had to choose something there. I didn't want to seem like I was ungrateful or that I was wasting her time. I spotted a brown velvet, two-piece top and long skirt that I liked, so I asked the designers to adapt the design into a long, one-piece, white velvet dress. It was perfect!

Just after 5:00 p.m. on February 4, 1977, I touched my mother's elegant diamond-and-ruby leaf that was pinned to my velvet dress, clutched my lilies-of-the-valley bouquet, and walked down the living room "aisle" with my father. Though it wasn't the big church wedding of my dreams, all the people I loved were there, so I was content. Billy and I each had only one attendant: my sister, Heidi, served as the maid of honor, and Billy's dad was his best man. Interestingly, although the Roses did not allow a church wedding, they had no problem with the minister from my childhood church performing the ceremony. Besides our families, several people attended the ceremony, including our friend George Steinbrenner, and one hundred more friends crowded into the apartment for the reception.

Billy and I left the reception after about two hours and headed straight to the airport to fly to Los Angeles. We spent the night at the Beverly Hills Hotel, a gift from Ann and Kirk Douglas, dear friends of Billy's parents who became "second parents" to Billy and eventually godparents to our son, Douglas, and then headed off for a week at the Racquet Club in Palm Springs. I remember climbing into bed that first night and being so excited to be Mrs. Billy Rose. What I didn't realize was that less than twelve hours earlier Billy had arrived at his parents' apartment—just upstairs from my father's own apartment—and said, "I can't go through with this." It was almost as if he had known how difficult the road ahead would be. However, his mom calmed him down and convinced him to carry through with the wedding.

Billy and I married despite the fact that we had absolutely no interests in common. I entered into marriage thinking that he would buy me happiness, that he would bring me the joy that I thought magically appears when you get married. But I was also scared going into marriage. I remember telling my best friend, Serena, that I didn't really think it would work because we had nothing in common. But I just wanted to be married; I thought it would fill that void of family that had been lost when my mom died. I figured we could always just get a divorce sometime down the road.

Chapter 3

AND BABY
MAKES THREE

UNSURPRISINGLY, OUR MARRIAGE got off to a rocky start.
We did not have a solid foundation, and I, for one, was not necessarily in it for the long haul. A strong marriage takes a firm commitment to God, to each other, and to making things work, and Billy and
I did not have that kind of mutual devotion to our relationship or any
kind of relationship with the Lord.

During those early days of marriage, I worked hard as a way to
hide my frustrations about the differences between Billy and me.
Marriage wasn't turning out to be all I'd thought. Being husband and
wife didn't change the fact that we were two very different people with
very opposite interests. Like many newlyweds, I had believed things
would change after the wedding and life settled into more of a routine. I had thought that once we were married, we would do some of
the things Billy liked and some of the things I liked. That wasn't the
case. We continued to do everything Billy liked—all of which had to
do with sports—and nothing that I liked. But I begrudgingly put up
with it because it was still more important to me to be married than to
be myself.

NEW YORK PARTY GIRL

Things went from bad to worse in the Rose household, and we separated one summer early in our marriage. I was extremely unhappy, and
I knew I needed to try to figure things out. The marriage wasn't working, and Billy was in his own world nearly all the time. I was extremely
frustrated with him and with the entire situation. I wanted out; if my
husband wasn't going to give me the attention and sense of fulfillment
I desired, I was going to see what else the world had to offer me.

When I told Billy I was leaving, he begged me to stay, but I refused. As far as I could see, I meant nothing to him. He pleaded all
night, but I felt like I was suffocating and just had to get out of there.
I moved back into my dad's place for a few weeks, and then I sublet a
studio apartment. I had a lot of fun that summer. Looking back, it's
hard to imagine that having an affair and trying cocaine for the first
time were what I considered to be fun, but for the first time I was free
to do whatever I wanted. I didn't consider the consequences of any
of my actions. In the meantime, Billy also started doing cocaine. He
was into it so heavily that he lost thirty pounds that summer—and I
thought he looked amazing!

Some friends called me one day at the end of the summer and said
they had just returned home from Bermuda, where they had seen Billy
with another woman. I told them not to tell me about it. I didn't want
to hear it; I was moving on. I truly believed I was. I had dated another
man. I had even told my boss at Saks that I was a single woman now
and supporting myself and therefore needed a raise, which they gave
me.

However, the day after I received that phone call, Billy called me.
He was in tears and said he had to see me. I was confused because I
thought he was happily vacationing in Bermuda with another woman.
He told me he was coming back early because all he could do was think
about me. He begged to get together that night, so we had dinner, and
he took me out for a horse-and-buggy ride. Billy said he realized he

hadn't been a good husband, but he wanted me back. He didn't want to be with another woman; he wanted us to be together. After listening to his plea, I agreed to move back home.

At that point we became entrenched in the New York party scene, which was unstoppable. We would go to Studio 54, stay until 4 a.m., and think nothing of it. The two of us would sit around with all sorts of famous people, doing lines of cocaine. In the late seventies, cocaine was just a fun thing to do; we didn't know that it was highly addictive—and addicted we became. I got very sick after about four months of our intense partying and drug use and realized I needed to stop. Billy didn't want to stop using. The truth was, he was so far gone that he couldn't stop. He kept saying it wasn't a problem, that he could do it when he wanted and not do it when he didn't, which I later learned is a classic sign of an addict. However, I knew nothing about addiction at the time, and I wanted to believe Billy, so I did nothing to try to stop him.

My work had suffered during those months of hard partying, and when I was using cocaine I didn't care, but I really *did* care. I loved my job and wanted to keep it, but I knew that could only happen if I stopped the cocaine use. I also knew that if I stayed in the party scene and around Billy all the time, I wouldn't be able to stay away from the drugs long enough to get clean. As a result, I asked Saks to send me to Florida for a short work trip. After a few days of work, I stayed in the hotel for the weekend so I could detox. It worked for the most part—I didn't crave it as I had before—but since it was still a huge part of Billy's life and our social life, I was still around it once I got home, and I fell back into old habits from time to time.

One of those nights, I ingested so much cocaine that I needed two Valium to get to sleep. Two weeks later I learned I was pregnant, and I realized I had been pregnant on that drug-filled night. I was distraught and very scared; I had done so many drugs that night that I was afraid I had damaged the baby. Though we hadn't been trying to get pregnant at the time, I didn't want to hurt the life that was growing inside me.

At fourteen weeks I started to bleed. After two long days, the doctor admitted me to the hospital. I waited much of the next day to have a sonogram, which determined the fetus had no heartbeat. My baby was dead. Was it because of the drugs? I don't know, but I'll always wonder if that was a factor.

I didn't know how to grieve the loss, because when I was growing up, my family didn't talk about our feelings or grief, which was evident in the way we reacted to my mother's death. I didn't know how to say that it was tearing me apart, but I knew I needed help, and I needed a distraction, so I talked Billy into buying a seven-week-old beagle puppy. We named him Homer in homage to Billy's baseball past.

AN ADDITION TO THE FAMILY

After the miscarriage, I desperately wanted to get pregnant again, and to my surprise, Billy was on board. The doctor told me to wait three months, and I took him at his word. Ninety days later, I was expecting again. I was worried that I would have another miscarriage, so I requested that my ob-gyn sign off on my taking the full nine months off from work at Saks. Though I didn't qualify as a high-risk pregnancy, the doctor agreed. This meant giving up my position at work, though I did expect to return to Saks in some capacity after the baby was born.

I was very sick during the first three months of the pregnancy, but I began feeling better around the sixteen-week mark. At that point I believed my baby would be safe and healthy, so I started doing volunteer work at my alma mater, the Spence School in Manhattan, and at my college in Boston. My other daily activities included housebreaking Homer, going to lunch with Billy's mom or my sister, visiting Billy at his office in the garment center, and watching daytime TV game shows. What a life I led—the typical New York wife's routine of lunches, charity work, and at times general idleness. If my bosses from Saks could have seen me, they would definitely have questioned my commitment to my job.

But I wasn't worried about work; I was thinking about how to prepare for my baby's arrival. We had to reclaim our second bedroom to use as a nursery. Up until that time, the room had served as a den and TV room and Billy's closet, but I managed to turn it into a beautiful new abode for our baby. I had a mural painted in the room that made us feel as if we were out in nature, with trees, birds, and animals galore. The closet doors were painted to look like green fields, with a castle and a picture of Homer in the corner. I also set up a daybed for the nurse we would hire to help out with our family's new addition.

While I had the amazing nursery and top-of-the-line accessories and clothes for my baby, I had absolutely no idea how to be a mom or take care of a baby. I hadn't done much babysitting, so I really was clueless. However, that wasn't what concerned me in the weeks leading up to the birth. I didn't even know enough to realize that I knew nothing about raising a child! Instead, I was consumed with the externals: my clothes, the baby's clothes, how to make the nursery even better, what we would do without a den and TV room, and more. Looking back, I wish I'd had someone to turn to who could have helped me as I ventured into the unknown world of motherhood, but I'm not sure I would have listened to anyone anyway.

The big day finally arrived, and we rushed to the hospital. Billy was not allowed in the delivery room, as was the custom in those days. After more than twenty-four hours of labor, the doctor ordered an emergency C-section, and Douglas William Rose entered the world on May 27, 1982, at 2:25 a.m.

When I was in recovery after the surgery, Billy came in and stayed about an hour. He then left me there on my own as I was moved to a ward with twelve beds. I couldn't move and was in terrible pain, my baby was off in the nursery, and I had nobody to help or comfort me. My dad came to visit several hours later, and he was excited to meet his new grandson, albeit through the nursery window. Later that day I was moved to a private room, but I was still in great pain, and the pain medication did not agree with me. I was unable to hold Douglas, which, as you can imagine, was difficult for a brand-new mother.

Billy did come back to see me, but the afternoon after Douglas was born, Billy had a softball playoff game, so he was off again. After the game, he and his best friend Richard stopped by the hospital, still in their uniforms, so they could see and hold Douglas. We also asked Richard to be a godfather to Douglas, and he readily agreed. I can vividly remember Billy sitting in the chair in the hospital room, holding his son and saying, "I promise to take care of you for the rest of my life."

EVERYTHING CHANGED—
BUT IT WAS STILL THE SAME

We hired a baby nurse to live with us full-time for the first month of Douglas's life, but we ended up keeping her on for three months. She was helpful to this new mother, who was clueless about parenting. The nurse would do night duty, bottle-feeding Douglas, who had been jaundiced and needed more supplement than I was able to provide by nursing.

During those first months, I woke during the night to Douglas's cries. I stayed in bed, knowing the nurse would care for him, but I lay awake feeling conflicted. Since I was the mom, I felt that I should be caring for my child, but I was so exhausted. I wondered what I had done in deciding to have a child. I felt very alone, and Billy was in no way involved with caring for Douglas. He had no idea about parenting either, and he really wasn't interested. He was used to watching sports whenever he was home, and that didn't stop once the baby was born. Since the nurse was there to care for Douglas, Billy felt he shouldn't have to help out. We both had much fear about this new stage of our lives, and we had no coping skills or supportive friends or family to help us deal with our fear and differences in opinion about who was responsible for child care. We also did not communicate with each other about any of it.

Six weeks after Douglas's birth, Billy insisted that he and I go to Bermuda with some friends. I did *not* want to leave Douglas so that we could go on vacation, but Billy was adamant, so we went. I was unhappy being away from my new baby, and I also didn't like being out in public on a tropical vacation before losing my baby weight.

By the time Douglas was three months old, I really wanted to care for him alone, and I wanted our family privacy back. Billy was reluctant to let the baby nurse go, but we finally did it. However, we did hire a housekeeper-nanny to help out two days a week.

I had become a critical person, just as my mother had been, and that first worker never did enough to please me. (In fact, I was never satisfied with anything in those days.) She lasted about ten months before I fired her. Then I hired Hazel, who brought much-needed joy into our lives. She loved Douglas, and she always had a smile on her face. Hazel commuted from Brooklyn, where she had a husband and child of her own. Looking back at the disparity of our lives, it's a bit of a shock. Hazel had to leave her child so she could come work for me, a woman who was home full-time with her baby. But that was just part of the lifestyle I had become used to.

Meanwhile, Billy worked all day and then came home to plop himself in front of the TV to watch whatever game was on, while doing lines of cocaine. Baseball, football, basketball, hockey—it didn't matter what sport it was. He watched anything that was on TV. Billy's mood followed his favorite teams' wins and losses. He was ecstatic when they won and miserable when they lost. It was like living on a roller coaster. I longed for a calm life and for Billy to pay attention to Douglas and me, not to his sports. But I was still afraid to do anything contrary to what Billy wanted. He was used to getting his own way, and I continued to let him. Although my marriage was unbelievably rocky, I still craved the lifestyle it afforded me, and I still believed that somehow, someday, I would finally figure out a way to be happy, so I did what I thought I needed to do—or not do—to keep my marriage intact.

Chapter 4

A TOUGH DECISION

SINCE MY HUSBAND WASN'T interested in spending time with me and our child, I was desperate to get out of the house and find someone else to spend time with and something else to do. Not long after Douglas was born, I reconnected with Donna, one of my childhood friends. Donna had given birth to her first baby, Hillary, three months before Douglas was born. The four of us became inseparable.

Donna's husband was in rehab for drugs, and since Billy was consumed by sports and not interested in doing anything with me or Douglas, the two of us were both basically on our own. It was great to get out of our apartment, to be able to do the things *I* wanted to do (with someone who wanted to do them with me!), and to have someone to commiserate with about our absent husbands. Donna and I spent our weekends going on outings with our babies. We would go to the Bronx Zoo, to museums, and to the park, and we'd even drive two hours to go outlet shopping in New Jersey. I don't know what I would have done without Donna at that stage of my life.

By that time, I was also a member of the alumnae board at my school in New York City, and I was on the board of trustees at Pine Manor College as a member of the visiting committee on business management. I felt completely unqualified for both of those posts. I had a feeling they had asked me to serve because they thought I had

lots of money to give, but I didn't. We appeared as though we had
money because we were part owners of the Yankees, but Billy's dad had
put up all the money. And while we had a housekeeper-nanny, and I
walked around in expensive clothes, they were paid for with money
from Billy's mom. I felt like a fraud.

A NEW START?

While I was getting ready for one of those meetings in March of
1984, I got an unexpected phone call from my ob-gyn. I was pregnant.
The baby was due in December. Once again I was extremely sick for
the first three months. With a toddler in the house, this was tougher
than before, but by that time Hazel was working five days a week.
Thankfully she was there for Douglas, because the time went by in a
blur. However, I dreaded weekends because Hazel wasn't there, and
Billy was absolutely no help.

One day early in my pregnancy, Billy got out of bed in the middle
of the night, took all of his cocaine stash, and dumped it in the toilet.
He decided he was going to kick his ever-growing habit, and I was
excited. I had known it was a problem, but I had no idea how to fix
his drug addiction, and he wouldn't have listened to me even if I had
known. Therefore, I was extremely glad he had decided to do it on his
own. Since it was his choice, he would be more likely to stick with it.

As part of this life change, Billy also changed careers. After working in the family textile business for ten years, he was tired of being in a
job he wasn't passionate about, so he decided to open a sports bar and
restaurant. He didn't consult me on the matter, which was normal in
our relationship in those days. He just said he was going to do it and,
true to form, I jumped on board without any questions or disagree-
ment and did my best to be the supportive wife.

Along with a friend, Billy leased a six-thousand-square-foot restaurant space in Tribeca, a yet undeveloped section of New York City in
Lower Manhattan, near Wall Street and the World Trade Center. We

spent six months renovating the space, going exactly five times over our original budget.

One of the biggest expenses came when Billy decided he wanted a state-of-the-art scoreboard like those found in Las Vegas that update scores in all sports as they happen. That was a big deal in the pre-Internet days, and nobody outside of Vegas had one of those boards, partly due to the fact that they cost $120,000! Accounting for inflation, that would be more than a quarter of a million dollars today—not a big deal for a major corporation, but this was a privately owned bar. Also, since the scoreboard used such specialized technology, nobody in the city, the state, or even the Eastern Seaboard could fix it, so we would have to fly people in from Cedar Rapids, Iowa, every time something broke. It was a costly endeavor, to say the least.

Billy's goal was to create an atmosphere in the restaurant such that people wouldn't want to *not* come for fear they would miss out on seeing some famous athlete. He started a celebrity bartending night where he would bring in a Knick, a Net, a Ranger, a Yankee, or a Met to tend bar during *Monday Night Football*. He also sought out college alumni groups to come watch their alma maters' games at the Sporting Club—and spend a lot of money on food and alcohol. These promotions and others helped to make the venture a success.

The Sporting Club opened in October of 1984, and as we drew near to opening, I realized that Billy had no experience with budgets or keeping track of merchandise. Due to my work at Saks, I was able to take over as bookkeeper. However, I had no experience in restaurant management, I was seven months pregnant, and Billy and I soon figured out that we did not work well together. I was used to running the show with my own department at Saks, but Billy did not like to be told what to do, especially by his usually compliant wife! We were in over our heads, and it was all a prescription for disaster. Anyone who has ever worked with a spouse knows that it is not the easiest thing in the world, even in the best of situations. Needless to say, we were a worst-case scenario.

We finally hired a real bookkeeper so I could return home to be with Douglas and wait for the baby's arrival. You would think I would have enjoyed the break, but it was an extremely difficult time. Billy was totally consumed by the restaurant. He would go into work around noon and not return home until 2:00 or 3:00 a.m., just to turn around and do it again the next day. He had no time or energy for anyone or anything other than the Sporting Club. He was exhausted and began acting erratic, and I suspected he had gone back to cocaine. I tried to be strong, but I actually felt very much alone.

A DESIRE FOR NORMALITY

Courtney Gage Rose arrived on December 18, 1984, at 8:05 a.m. at Lenox Hill Hospital. She was beautiful with fair skin, dark hair, and blue eyes. Billy was there for an hour after Courtney's birth, but then he left for the Sporting Club's first press conference, held for the arrival of the New York Yankees' newest player, Rickey Henderson. Billy came to the hospital again only rarely to visit his wife and new daughter. It seemed as if his loyalty was still with sports and his restaurant, not with our family.

When I'd headed to the hospital for the C-section, I'd left Douglas in the care of Hazel. However, Hazel was only available during the day on weekdays, and since Billy had no time or inclination to take care of two-and-a-half-year-old Douglas, we had to hire another sitter to come and stay with him during my six-day hospital stay. I felt horrible leaving Douglas with a woman he didn't know, and he felt completely abandoned. For nearly a week he saw neither his father nor his mother, who was usually with him all the time. When I came home, he was angry, yet he didn't want to leave my side. However, I was still recovering from my surgery and was trying to take care of a newborn, so I wasn't much comfort to him. Meanwhile, Billy was oblivious to it all.

I was insecure as a mom, and because of Douglas's temperament, I couldn't do the things that other moms did. He was constantly in motion, and I didn't know how to take care of him. I just wished he would stay still and play quietly, but that was only a pipe dream. My son had no interest in being anything but a boisterous boy. Courtney, on the other hand, was extremely laid back and calm. Those differences made me start thinking about how there was someone outside of me who had created these children. I didn't go so far as to think it might be the Creator, but I knew it was something bigger than I. Something else was at work in the world, and I had no control over it.

Our first Christmas as a family of four, just seven days after Courtney's birth, was difficult at best. Billy slept almost all day, the baby nurse was there, and my whole family stopped by to bring gifts. I was completely exhausted, and I cried a lot. What a way to spend my daughter's first Christmas!

Just a few weeks later, when the weather turned unseasonably warm, I remember taking Douglas and Courtney to the park together for the first time. I was just a few weeks out of surgery, and I was alone with my children, but I was also full of joy about being able to get out of the house with my two babies. Often on these outings I saw couples with their children and looked at them longingly, wishing so badly that Billy could be with us. I just wanted us to be a normal family doing things that normal families do together.

IS THIS ALL THERE IS?

A year and a half after Courtney's birth, I was lying on a beach chair in Hilton Head, South Carolina. I sat alone, staring out at the ocean with tears streaming down my face. I asked a God I didn't know, "Is this all there is? Is this really what life and marriage are all about?" My husband of nine years was sleeping in our hotel room in the middle of a beautiful, sunny day. Meanwhile, I watched couples running up and down the beach, some playing Frisbee, others paddleball. Children were swimming, splashing, and shouting gleefully. They were laughing and having fun all around me while I sat there alone and crying, hopeless, and in a deep despair.

Billy was sleeping because he was trying to detox his body from its powerful addiction to cocaine. My earlier suspicions had proven true. My husband had gotten back into drugs, and they were completely controlling his life and making our family miserable. Our active, precocious, and precious four-year-old son and beautiful, serene one-and-a-half-year-old baby daughter were at home in New York City with our babysitter. I was beyond despondent and didn't know where to turn. Billy refused to seek professional help for his problem, and I had no idea how to help him. I had spent the last six years covering up his erratic, moody, irresponsible behavior, and I was now at the end of my abilities. I hoped that what had worked for me would work for him— getting away from the drugs and the party culture long enough to get it all out of his system.

As he slept, I thought about our marriage. We had no life together; it was as if we were living two separate lives while living in the same small, crowded apartment. Billy's life was completely centered on the Sporting Club. He was still keeping a ridiculous work schedule, typically working twelve- to fourteen-hour days, starting in the early to middle afternoon. He usually woke up and left the house about the same time I came home from preschool with Douglas. Often we were accompanied by one of Douglas's little friends and the other child's mom. Billy, too strung out to know or care about anything the kids and I were doing, would stumble out of the apartment without even saying hello to my guests. I was completely embarrassed by his behavior, but I continued to put up with it, to no one's surprise.

I actually thought that maybe our marriage and family were so messed up because something was wrong with me. Was I not a good enough wife for Billy? Did I not meet his expectations? Did he wish he had a different—a better—life? Was that why he put drugs before his family?

So while sitting there on the beach, I thought, *There has to be more to life than this. What is life all about?* I was so lonely. I had finally realized that all the things and people in the world would never make me happy, but I didn't know what would.

In spite of the fact that I did not want to be separated—or, for that matter, divorced—and was terrified and anxious about how I would financially support my kids and parent them alone, two weeks after we returned to New York, I asked Billy to leave. I told him I loved him, but I couldn't live the way we did anymore. He was still snorting cocaine regularly and wouldn't discuss the situation with me, and nothing had really changed. He was entrenched in his "I'll handle this myself in my own way" mode. I had reached my limit in our travesty of a marriage. I told him to get himself cleaned up and get his life back on track, and then he could come back. Little did I know just how long that would take.

Chapter 5

ON MY OWN

IT WOULD HAVE BEEN EASY TO BLAME Billy for the demise of our marriage. After all, he had a huge drug problem and was very controlling. But I definitely had my part to play in our separation. I had just felt such emptiness when Billy and things didn't fill the hole inside of me. The problem is that when you try to fill your life with people and things, nothing is ever enough. I'd get a new handbag, and I'd want three more of them.

It was similar to the time earlier in my life when I had leaned on the stability and status of my job as a fashion buyer with a $10 million budget. Outside my 5th Avenue office window, I had a view of Rockefeller Center. I remember looking out at that view and arrogantly thinking, *If I work really hard, I could be president of this store one day.* But at the same time I thought, *What would that do?* For a month or so, everyone would think I was wonderful, and then it would just be a really hard grind, and I'd be back to where I was.

Whatever it is you get—whether it's a brand-new, beautiful pair of designer shoes or the corner office—a month later, an hour later, or five minutes later, the emptiness is right back. It's fun to buy things and to get dressed up in them for a short time, but then you're right back where you started. And with a job, what happens when you get to the top—when there's nowhere else to go, no other obstacles to overcome to get to that next level? It takes away your drive.

I had been a discontented wife and had really put the responsibility for that on my husband. I thought it was his fault. Yet in some ways I felt that his problems were my fault, that I had driven him to drugs. I knew he'd made his own choices, but I was filled with discontentment, and that is never a good thing for a wife. It doesn't help you support, respect, or encourage your husband, and it makes him feel that he's never providing enough, never good enough.

FACING FAILURE

The day after Billy moved out, his mother took me to a twelve-step recovery program that helps family members of people with addictions. I learned what addiction is all about and how my unhealthy relationship with and dependence upon Billy and my utter willingness to compromise on his behalf (without him compromising on my behalf) had contributed to the problem. We had both tried to control each other in our own ways, and I had compromised almost everything I believed, needed, liked, and enjoyed, including my friends and interests.

Working through these issues helped me realize there were other people in my situation; I was not alone. As I learned the twelve steps, I began to think about a higher power and to surrender to it.[2] I wondered who that higher power really was. I had gone to church as a child, so I knew a little about God, but I really didn't know who He was or what He did, and I never dreamed that He might actually care about me. If there was a God, wouldn't He have much bigger problems to worry about than my life and marriage?

Though I didn't realize it at the time, God was in the process of drawing me to Himself. He had plans for my life, for Billy's life, for our marriage and family, that I couldn't imagine at that low point in my life. I cried a lot during those days. I would wonder, *How am I going to raise my two children by myself? How am I going to afford it? How am I going to physically do it?* I had technically been doing much of that already—Billy had never taken on any sort of parenting role—but it was different being completely on my own. I felt like such a failure. I had failed at marriage, I had failed at getting my husband to stop doing drugs, and I had failed at being a parent to my two precious children.

Interestingly enough, not long after the separation, Billy's mom suggested that I have an affair as a way to move past my unhappiness, and I went along with it. A willing friend fixed me up with a single doctor. After several weeks, I realized this affair wasn't for me and that an affair was definitely not the answer. Though I was sure Billy was sleeping with other women, being unfaithful to him wasn't making things any better. It did not bring me any peace or joy; instead, it only added more chaos to my already turbulent heart and made me lonelier than ever.

Soon after the separation, Douglas began having problems at preschool, and the school recommended I send him to a child psychologist. The psychologist, thankfully, saw my need for counseling as well and insisted I resume my therapy. I had begun going to therapy during my first separation from Billy, and it had been helpful. I had been able to talk about my mother for the first time and begin to work through my childhood issues and my grief over her death. But after the second separation, I kept insisting I was fine even though I was falling apart. I did finally agree to start seeing a counselor again.

I also began to journal my thoughts and feelings. Here's an excerpt from that time:

June 26, 1986

I woke up this morning feeling kind of anxious. It's like I wake up, think for a minute, and this feeling grabs me. It's fear. I'm going to see Billy today at my request. My feelings are so jumbled about him—love, hate, anger, comfort. I want to put away for later any decisions, until I am whole.

So while I did begin to work through the issues surrounding my imploded marriage, things were definitely not great. I still experienced times of great loneliness, stress, and fear, and I didn't know how to get rid of them.

December 1986

> One thing that's very clear to me is that I have absolutely no idea of who I am; I have no direction. I feel scared and anxious and bare to the bone. All these months of working with a therapist, and I feel more muddled than ever.

The twelve-step program and therapy did help some, but they didn't technically solve any of my problems—nothing but Jesus would be able to do that. They just helped me to better understand the issues.

FINDING MARY POPPINS

One year later, in May 1987, still separated but not divorced, I went back to work to help support my family. Billy kept telling me he could not afford to support me anymore and that I needed to find a job. So after several interviews, including one with Saks Fifth Avenue, I finally landed a job with Puritan Men's Clothing, a men's shirting company.

On my first day back to work, my last view of Courtney was her tearstained face next to the new nanny, Pansy, at the top of the subway steps. I also cried all the way to my new job. I was heartbroken, confused, angry, and sad about having to leave my children at home, but I knew I had to get back to work. At the same time, however, I thought maybe they'd be better off with a Mary Poppins than with their failure of a mother.

It took four nannies to find one remotely close to Mary Poppins. The first, a young Irish au pair, gave Courtney three teaspoons of medicine one day, thinking that two-thirds of a teaspoon meant two or three teaspoons. When I returned home and learned about the medicine overdose, I frantically called the pediatrician and was told to administer ipecac syrup immediately to cause Courtney to throw up. If you have ever had the misfortune of forcing your child to drink this horrible-tasting syrup, you know it's like torturing your child and is a horrendous ordeal!

The next nanny took Douglas and Courtney to the supermarket in the double stroller. She left them outside the market in the middle of New York City and asked five-year-old Douglas to watch his two-and-a-half-year-old sister. You'd think I would have fired her on the spot when Douglas told me about this scary episode, but I knew I would have to miss work if I let her go, so I didn't have the courage to fire her for three more weeks. I was definitely in a mixed-up and fear-filled state at the time.

Another nanny began, but after one week she phoned me on Sunday night from the hospital. Her boyfriend had beaten her and broken her right arm, so she'd be unable to work for a month or two. There I was, scrambling again for someone to watch the kids while I went to work. A friend came for two days, and my sister also helped out until I could hire another nanny.

Finally, Mary (last name not Poppins) arrived. She was another young, Irish girl who truly loved the kids, though she did play favorites. After three months on the job, she told me she needed Mondays off. By then we were all dependent on Mary, and I didn't want to fire her and hire yet another nanny, so my upstairs neighbor Frances, an older, retired schoolteacher, became the Monday sitter.

Life was chaotic during those years. Nannies were coming and going, and I had to scramble to be home when they weren't available. My work schedule was 9:00 a.m. to 5:30 p.m. None of my coworkers had children, and they stayed much later, but before I was hired, I'd told my boss that because of my situation as a single parent, I'd be able to work only those specific hours, and he'd agreed to it. I would race home by subway, and as long as the trains were moving on time, I was home in time for Mary to leave at 6:00. By the time I arrived, she'd have the kids bathed and ready for bed, and she was ready to walk out the door. After fixing and eating dinner with Douglas and Courtney, I'd put them to bed and then fall into my own empty bed, dreaming of a time when life wouldn't be so crazy.

WORK AND WORRIES

My job at Puritan did not go well. When I was hired, they'd told me I would be a merchandise stylist, helping to give fashion input to their designs. Instead they gave me computer spreadsheets to tally and track merchandise movement under the direction of a woman I'll call Candy. Candy did not like me and had not wanted the company to hire me. In short, she made my life miserable.

In fact, every part of that job was miserable. En route to one of Puritan's factories in a small town in Pennsylvania, we flew through a terrible storm, and I was sure our small prop plane was going to crash and that I was going to die. I clung desperately to my seat and prayed to that higher power I really didn't know. Back in New York City three days later, when I was on my way home from the airport, the taxi skidded in the rain and spun in circles through the Central Park transverse, finally crashing to a stop. Very shaken but physically uninjured, I couldn't believe all that was happening. Though I had written in my journal only five months earlier, "The consistency of a job would be wonderful," this was not proving to be true at all.

That July the company was holding its preseason rally meetings at a hotel near LaGuardia Airport. The meeting lasted two days, and I had to share a hotel room with three other female employees. On the way home in a taxi with one of my roommates, I looked over on the highway and saw Billy driving our BMW. He and a friend were on their way home from the beach. I was so angry at my situation. There he was, driving around in a fancy car going to the beach, while I'd been sharing a hotel room with three other women at a men's shirt rally and leaving my children at home with a sitter. It was more than I could bear!

After three months at Puritan, I finally called my former boss at

Saks, who had become a vice president at Macy's corporate office, to discuss other job possibilities. The lunch went well, and I was offered a job as a buyer in Macy's corporate dress division. This job required me to travel to Hong Kong, Taipei, Seoul, Singapore, and Tokyo. The first trip was scheduled soon after I began the new job. Even though it meant leaving my children at home with a nanny for two weeks at a time, I was actually thrilled to go and visit these exotic countries. It seemed as though it would be a rest and vacation from home life.

The trips were refreshing, yes, but definitely not a vacation. We worked hard and long hours, visiting all the factories that produced our dresses and then dining afterward with our manufacturers. The twelve-hour time difference was also a difficult adjustment. On the positive side, everything we did on the trip was expensed; we ate in excellent restaurants and stayed in four-star hotels. The trip was definitely a break from the grinding routine of daily life as a single parent with limited financial resources, but I was just anxious to be home with my children, eating chicken fingers and canned peas and doing laundry in the basement of our apartment building.

At the end of the long two-week trip, coming into Kennedy Airport after a fourteen-hour flight from Hong Kong, I was focused on two things. The first was my concern that customs would confiscate the four knockoff Fendi pocketbooks that I had purchased in Seoul for ten dollars each for my stepmother to give as gifts. The second was a rising hope that Billy would meet me at the airport with Douglas and Courtney. At this point, we had been separated for one and a half years. I was still hoping for something that totally did not exist. I had no reason whatsoever to expect Billy to be there. I just still yearned for my family to be together. So when I exited customs (pocketbooks still in hand) and found no one there to meet me, a sadness and loneliness pervaded every part of my being. As I found a cab, stark reality set in. But little did I know what I would face when I reached home.

When I arrived back at the apartment, I found that Douglas had fallen from his top bunk bed onto his head two days earlier. He had suffered a seizure and landed in intensive care for a night. Though Billy met Douglas and the babysitter at the hospital and interceded for our son, not allowing the doctors to give Douglas an unnecessary intravenous tube, it was the babysitter who had stayed overnight with Douglas, while her boyfriend stayed at home with Courtney. My hopes for reconciliation with my husband were crushed even further. I wasn't sure we could ever get out of the hole we were in.

Chapter 6

NEW LIFE

IT SEEMED THAT THE CHAOS WAS escalating and the hole was getting even deeper. Billy was still completely absorbed with the restaurant and now was so involved with another woman that they were living together just three blocks away from our apartment. When I had a medical emergency just a week later, I was all alone—again.

A week after I returned from the trip, I ended up in the hospital on intravenous antibiotics with a severely infected thumb. I had nursed my thumb myself for a week, having no spare time to visit the doctor. But by Friday afternoon, I realized the swelling on my thumb, now the size of a large grape, was getting serious.

I called our family doctor, and he agreed to wait for me until I got off work. The doctor took one look at my thumb and said it was serious and needed surgery. However, the only surgeon he could find still in the office at 5:30 on a Friday evening was an orthopedist who had just finished his internship and was new to the practice. The surgeon looked at my thumb and said I needed to be admitted to the hospital that very moment. He was concerned that the infection would red-line to my heart and prove fatal. I explained that I was a single parent of two preschoolers and that I had to go home and make arrangements for them. So he insisted that he do an immediate in-office surgery to try to drain the infection. After the painful procedure, the doctor reiterated my need to be in the hospital because, without a full surgical anesthesia block on my arm, he was unable to get all the infection.

I phoned Billy and explained the situation. He was angry with me for asking him to help and said there was no possible way he could leave the restaurant and take care of our children. So I went home, against the doctor's wishes, to find someone to stay with the kids. I literally begged Mary to give up her weekend and stay, and she finally agreed. I headed back to the hospital to be admitted through the emergency room. I was by myself, which seemed to be a running theme during those days. My father and stepmother were out of town and unreachable. My sister and her husband were facing infertility, and this was the weekend they needed to stay at home to administer special shots at specific times around the clock, so they couldn't come either. Our friends Richard and Lisa were able to come for a short time on Saturday morning, bringing me magazines and lamenting my situation. I was in a room with an older woman who was receiving chemo for bone cancer, and there I was, carrying on because of an infected thumb. Even I felt badly that I was causing such a scene.

I felt so alone. I couldn't believe I was in the hospital, and I was totally miserable, frightened, and angry. What on earth was happening to my life? This wasn't part of the picture I had imagined when I said, "I do." I felt lost and abandoned, and my life was spinning out of control.

Billy did visit after the second surgery, bringing me a turkey sandwich and sitting with me for a half hour en route to work. Frankly, his visit only made me angry. Courtney and Douglas had also come to visit me in the hospital, but Courtney was afraid of my bandaged arm and couldn't wait to leave. A week later, after another surgery and lots of intravenous antibiotics, I was released and sent home.

A TIMELY INVITATION

When I finally came home from the hospital, an invitation was waiting for me in the mail. I had been invited to a black-tie dinner given by Mrs. Arthur S. DeMoss. United States Secretary of the Interior

Donald Hodel and his wife, Barbara, were to give a talk, "Christianity in the World Today," at the Waldorf Astoria Hotel. I thought, *I'm going. It's an opportunity to get dressed and go out!* I really wasn't that interested in the topic, but it was a dinner party and an opportunity to get out of the house for a social event without the kids. As a single mom, I didn't have much opportunity to do anything but take care of the kids and fall into bed exhausted, only to go to work the next day and start the cycle over again.

Though I didn't often get the chance to go out after the nanny had gone home, I did have a budget-friendly option for babysitting. My next-door neighbor had two young daughters who charged only three dollars an hour and were often available to babysit at the last minute. They even played with the kids at times, playing soccer in the long hallway of our apartment building outside our front door, giving me time to take a shower, write a letter, or clean house.

So when I had the opportunity to go to the dinner at the Waldorf Astoria, I jumped on it. The invitation also had a handwritten note in the corner from one of our former nannies. Debbie had been a waitress at the Sporting Club, and before Billy and I separated, I had "borrowed" her during a nanny crisis at home. We had her move in with us so she would be there at nights after Hazel had gone home, which allowed me time to spend evenings in the restaurant with Billy. Debbie was a fantastic nanny, the kids loved her, and there was something about her that was just different. She was always full of joy and would talk to me about God, which I thought was silly.

After a year of working for and living with us, Debbie went on to work for the DeMoss family, who planned formal events as a way to share the gospel with New York's elite. They would bring in big-name, sought-after speakers who would share their testimonies of God's work in their lives. Debbie sent me invitations, but I just threw them out, thinking the events weren't anything I would actually be interested in. One time I did accept, and then I forgot to go. When Debbie called me early that evening as I was giving the kids a bath, I realized that I hadn't looked at my calendar, and the event at the Waldorf had completely slipped my mind. She asked if I was coming, and I thought she would be angry that I had forgotten, because that was the way things went in New York, but she was actually very kind about it. It surprised me enough that when I received that next invitation, I made sure to go.

When I was dressed that night in a beautiful, black silk dress I had bought with my Macy's discount, I was shocked by how much I looked like the socialites in *Women's Wear Daily* and how that once-longed-for lifestyle had definitely not delivered. Though I looked the part, I was barely able to make ends meet and was unable to afford some of the fun things of which the glamorous New Yorkers partook, such as shows, charity fund-raisers, concerts for children, and taxicabs to get to those events. What truly amazed me, now that my desire was for a happy family and a loving husband, was that my look was totally a farce.

A NEW BEGINNING

My life completely changed that night in the grand ballroom at the Waldorf Astoria. Donald and Barbara Hodel shared things that I had never learned in all my childhood years in church or in my year and a half of twelve-step meetings talking about that higher power. They told me that God loved me and had a plan for my life, and that He wanted to have a personal relationship with me. They shared that mankind is sinful and separated from God because of sin.

I thought, *Well, in spite of the fact that I've wished my husband dead, I haven't killed him. So I'm really not a sinner.* But they explained that night that sin is anything such as worry or envy or gossip—things I engaged in all the time—and that all my self-centered choices were actually rebellion toward God. So maybe I was a sinner after all. Why hadn't I learned this in church when I was a child?

Thankfully, the Hodels didn't leave me hanging, thinking I was beyond redemption and that there was nothing I could do about it. The good news was that God sent His only Son, Jesus Christ, to live on this earth, die on a cross, and pay the penalty for my sin. Why did He do this? He did it because of His great love for and because God is the just judge, and there must be restitution for wrongs committed. Someone had to pay, and Jesus paid that price for all who believe. They explained that if I placed my faith in Jesus, then I would spend all eternity in heaven, and all my sins would be forgiven.

After the Hodels explained the gospel to the nine hundred people at that black-tie dinner in New York City, they said they were going to offer each of us an opportunity to pray and ask Jesus Christ into our life. It was as if God spoke directly to me. Parts of the Hodels' story matched my life. They had a son who was addicted to cocaine, and they shared all sorts of things that I could completely relate to. But the thing that I understood most that night—somewhat, but not fully—was that I wanted and needed Jesus Christ. I knew I was a sinner, even though I had managed not to kill my husband, and somebody had to pay. What a relief that I didn't have to pay the penalty myself—Jesus had done it for me!

I prayed when they offered the opportunity, and I asked Jesus to take over my life. I asked Him to make me be the person that He had created me to be. Then the Hodels extended an invitation to attend Bible study at the DeMoss House on East 73rd Street the following week. I couldn't get there fast enough. I felt as if a five-hundred-pound magnet was drawing me. In that newcomers' class, I began to learn all about the God of the Bible.

I discovered that the Bible is the inspired Word of God—the absolute truth. Jesus Christ is God's Son, the Messiah to the world, God Himself. Through knowing Him, I was given the gift of eternal life, which means I will spend all eternity with God. Finally, I knew He was the one to whom I could turn over my will, the one I could trust with all my problems. He was the one who could fill the emptiness in my heart, thus removing my longing for things. And He was the one who could give me great joy, even in the midst of unchanged circumstances, because of His great love. He was the answer, and His Word comforted my anxieties. As a single parent, I had many worries!

At this point, the first three steps of my twelve-step recovery program finally made sense and truly came to fruition. I had admitted I was powerless over addiction and that my life had become unmanageable. I came to believe that a power greater than me could restore my sanity. And I made a decision to turn my will and life over to the care of that higher power—the God who created the universe and rescued me from my sin.

I now believed not only that God had created me but also that I had become a new creation in Him. He had changed my life in so many ways, and I was extremely grateful. I wrote in my journal during my second work trip to Asia:

February 1988

> I feel so grateful for yesterday's day of rest and amazing church service here in Singapore. I am so thankful to feel God and Jesus in my life and to feel at peace. Thank You, God, through Jesus, for Your forgiveness and salvation and promise of eternal life.

I began to share the gospel with everyone I knew: my children, my sister and her husband, my father and stepmother, my neighbors, and even Billy. My neighbor Steve asked me if I had a new boyfriend, because I seemed so happy. And at breakfast every morning, I started reading *Leading Little Ones to God*, a children's devotional book, to Douglas and Courtney.[3] I wanted to share with them this incredible new joy I had received. We always ended our short study time with prayer.

One morning, Douglas suggested we pray for Daddy, and Courtney readily agreed. Frankly, I wanted to kill Daddy, not pray for him, but I didn't want to shape Douglas and Courtney's opinion of their father, so I agreed. And we began to pray daily for Daddy to come to know Jesus. Every morning at breakfast and every night at bedtime, Douglas and Courtney asked God for their daddy to come to know Jesus. Billy's salvation became my number-one prayer request in church, in Bible study, and to prayer hotlines. There were many, many people praying for Bill Rose, the man I'd taken to be my wedded husband—for better or for worse—eleven years earlier.

Chapter 7

WRESTLING WITH HARD TEACHINGS

AS I LEARNED MORE AND MORE ABOUT God and His Son, I became ever more excited about what I was discovering. These were life-changing principles I was reading in the Bible. I had been going to Bible study weekly, had begun reading the Bible daily, and was reading several extra Bible study books on my own, apart from the weekly group study. My insatiable hunger for the things of God had grown and grown. I had learned that God's Word is the truth and that Jesus is the way, the truth, and the life. I desperately wanted truth to be in my life (John 14:6), and I wanted to do things God's way instead of manipulating things to be my way. Up to that point, I had done everything in my life my own way, which I had finally realized was the reason for my current mess.

However, I soon ran into a problem that all new believers ultimately come up against—I found a teaching I didn't like. It didn't fit into what I wanted for my life and the direction I thought I was headed.

GOD'S VIEW OF DIVORCE

A few months after that significant dinner at the Waldorf Astoria, the DeMoss House offered a Saturday seminar on the topic of singles and dating, led by Christian counselor Jeff Stark. I couldn't sign up fast enough. I wanted to learn the Bible's ground rules for my new life in Christ and how that related to dating, since I was now single (at least in my mind, if not on paper). I was looking forward to finding out the best way to meet, get to know, and eventually marry a man who shared my new beliefs. Oh, how wonderful it would be to have a relationship with a Christian man! I imagined it would be *so* much better than being married to Billy Rose, who had crushed all my hopes and dreams about what life would be as a wife and mother.

By the end of the day, my excitement about the Bible's teaching on singleness was seriously depleted. I was shocked and extremely disappointed when I discovered that I was not single at all. From God's viewpoint, I was still married to Bill Rose, which meant no dating for Vicki Rose. This was incredibly hard to swallow. On my way home from work one day, I had seen Billy and the woman he was living with climbing into our car. I was taking the subway; Billy was driving our BMW with another woman. I couldn't stand it. It wasn't fair that he was moving on while I wasn't. And then I found out that because we weren't divorced or even legally separated, in God's eyes we were still married! Billy wasn't acting as though we were married, so why should I have to? I needed *out* of that marriage, and fast.

I made an appointment to see Jeff Stark. I needed clarification about this issue. I did not want to have to continue in a holding pattern while still married to Billy. I needed a divorce to get on with my life. But just as in the singles seminar, I was not at all excited about what I learned in my first session with Jeff:

- God hates divorce (Mal. 2:16).
- If I were to divorce my husband and remarry, in God's eyes I would be an adulterer (Matt. 5:32; Mark 10:11–12).
- The seventh of the Ten Commandments says, "You shall not commit adultery" (Ex. 20:14).
- "He answered, "Have you not read that he who created them from the beginning made them male and female . . . and . . .

'Therefore a man shall leave his father and his mother and hold fast to his wife, and the two shall become one flesh'? So they are no longer two but one flesh. What therefore God has joined together let not man separate" (Matt. 19:4–6; see also Mark 10:6–9).

- "For a married woman is bound by law to her husband while he lives, but if her husband dies she is released from the law of marriage" (Rom. 7:2).

I was stunned, speechless, and stuck! I had come to the place of wanting to obey God's Word 100 percent, because doing things my way hadn't worked at all, and because God is, well, *God*! God's Word is the truth, the answer to my every question, the only way to do anything, my authority, and now—for the first time in my new faith—very hard.

Jeff turned to Genesis 25 and showed me the story of Jacob and Esau as an example of the cost of demanding my own way. Esau, famished after hunting, asked his brother for a bowl of stew. Jacob agreed to feed his hungry older brother in exchange for the birthright, the inheritance traditionally given to the firstborn son. Esau agreed to his brother's request. Genesis 25:33 says, "So he [Esau] swore to him [Jacob], and sold his birthright to Jacob." And verse 34 says, "Thus Esau despised his birthright." For a mere bowl of stew, to satisfy his physical hunger, he gave up the promises of God in his life and the riches of his inheritance. This story is a vivid illustration and reminder that immediate indulgence is no substitute for holding on to what God desires and plans for us. Esau's self-centered habit of loving himself more than loving God brought him to this place. Beth Moore says, "The message of Esau's life has nothing to do with stew. It has to do with thinking so little about who you are that you'd forfeit a godly heritage for instant gratification."[4]

The application for me was so powerful. Was I willing to give up my obedient walk with God and all that God had planned for me just for a date with a man? Did I want instant gratification and a new husband more than I wanted to obey God by not dating and instead waiting on God's plan for my life to unfold in His way and time? My birthright, Jeff taught, is the abundant life (John 10:10) that God offers me if I obey Him and walk with Him. It is the riches of His glorious inheritance (Eph. 1:18).

So right then and there, I made a choice—God's way, not Vicki's. No more dating—to the point that a really handsome, young man from Bible study asked me to go to the philharmonic one night, and at first I thought, *Well, there's nothing wrong with that. It's just one night to have a little bit of fun with this guy from Bible study.* And so I accepted his invitation. Then I realized, with some help, that having one night of fun with this man wouldn't be honoring or pleasing to the Lord. I didn't want to go even slightly away from what His Word said.

So I called the guy and said, "I'm really sorry if I've hurt you in any way, but I really can't go out. I'm still married, and that's just not the right thing to do. And I really want to honor the Lord."

From my current standpoint, I can see how God has honored that feeble attempt at obedience by how He's blessed my life in terms of my reconciled marriage. If anyone reading this is struggling through something similar, wondering if just one date or one night out or one "something" isn't any big deal, in some ways it's not a big deal. But in the eyes of the Lord—who created the universe and who gave His Son to die so that you and I could be forgiven and spend all of eternity with Him—it's a big deal when we try to do what He says. And He blesses that (see Deut. 28:1–14).

However, in the moment, it had been hard to see without some help. It was also hard to see how I could bear to be stuck where I was— single, separated, working full-time in a job making ugly dresses that didn't sell—for the rest of my life. How would I raise my children to be godly if I was always working instead of being at home with them, teaching them the things of God? How would I tolerate my husband's antics? I didn't know the answers, and at first I didn't even want to think about them. The vision of my future in perpetual separation from my husband was almost too hard to bear.

Not long after becoming a Christian, I also started attending Bible teaching conferences. My first conference featured speaker Evelyn Christenson, author of the book *What Happens When Women Pray*.[5] She told story after story about her experiences of praying and of having people pray for her. I left that weekend so overwhelmed with the fact that God hears and answers prayer, loves us so much, and knows what we're going through. At that same conference I met Eleanor Page, a radio host and older, godly woman, who said to me, "My dear, once you are married, you are married for life." Yet another person was confirming God's will that I not divorce my husband.

I also realized that if I had to stay married to Billy, we likely wouldn't get back together unless he became a believer. So at that point I began more earnestly to pray for his salvation. That conference was a turning point in that regard. Eleanor Page's words stopped me in my tracks. This wasn't the first time I had heard similar words about marriage. And these words played a huge role in eventually turning my heart back toward my marriage, even though nothing had changed in Billy's life. Perchance Evelyn Christianson's way of prayer was my answer.

THE BLESSING OF GIVING

One Sunday not too long after my initial seminar with Jeff Stark, where I had learned what God said about divorce, I learned another hard lesson about the way God now wanted me to live my life as His follower. As I put my five dollars in the offering plate at church, the Lord impressed upon me, "Is five dollars really a tithe?" I thought that I was so noble putting five dollars in the plate each Sunday, considering my circumstances as a single, working mom. Yet I couldn't get away from thinking about the tithe. As a child, I had always given 10 percent of my allowance as an offering at church. I vividly remembered the numbered envelopes and the dimes and quarters I gave. However, since I hadn't known the Lord, my giving had been a habit, not an act of worship, gratitude, or love. With that in mind, it's no surprise that I stopped tithing when I went to college. But after seeking some godly counsel, I decided to start again and to do so in a spirit of trusting God.

This was so new for me. In the past, I had spent every dollar on myself—on my clothes, shoes, and things for the apartment, and the "right" clothes for the kids. And I never had money in the bank. I was always going to Billy for more. But once I began to tithe, I lost my desire for things, and I began to be grateful for everything: the food on our table, our small apartment that I suddenly viewed as a wonderful roof over our heads, the doormen who protected our building, central air-conditioning, the clothes in my closet, and so on. I began to see that God had provided all of it and that I had much more than I needed.

THE *HARD* IS WHAT MAKES IT GREAT

Looking back, I can see God's grace in waiting to teach me those lessons rather than doing so immediately after my conversion. He gave me time to get to know Him and discover His nature—His love, His kindness, His desire for my best, His sovereignty—before He brought the hard teachings to me. By the time I heard something I didn't like—or that my former self wouldn't like—I understood enough about Him and loved Him enough to obey, even if it wasn't what I wanted to hear. I knew my God well enough to realize that even His hard teachings are ultimately for my best and filtered through His great love for me.

I would like to wrap everything up in a little bow and say that once you love Jesus, even the hard things will be easy, but that's not always the case. But what I can tell you is that doing the hard things is worth it. Doing the hard things draws us closer to God, leads us to depend on Him, and builds character.

If you've ever seen the baseball movie *A League of Their Own*, you'll remember a scene in which one of the players tells the coach why she's quitting the team. "It just got too hard," she said. The coach replies, "It's supposed to be hard. If it wasn't hard, everyone would do it. The *hard* is what makes it great."[6] I could say the same about the life of a believer: the hard is what makes it great. The hard is what changes you. The hard is where you often see God most clearly.

Chapter 8

FORGIVENESS
AND PROVISION

IN JULY 1989, I WAS INTERVIEWED by Bill Bright, the late founder of Campus Crusade for Christ, at a staff-training ministry conference in Fort Collins, Colorado. In front of five thousand staff members, Dr. Bright and his associate asked me how I had come to know Christ and what subsequent changes had come about in my life. Two days later, while saying good-bye to Dr. Bright, he prayed that Billy would come to know Jesus Christ and that God would restore our marriage. A friend who was with me stated, "Well, Vicki, it's only a matter of time now until Billy comes to Christ, because when Dr. Bright prays, God answers." Many staff members also approached me over the course of my time in Fort Collins to tell me they would pray for Billy. And two weeks after I returned home, I received a call from a woman I didn't know, Charlotte Patrick. She had been at the conference, and she called to encourage me and to tell me that she, her family, and her Sunday school class would be praying for me and my marriage. The love and support of complete strangers overwhelmed me and gave me strength to persevere.

By that time, I very much wanted Billy to know the Savior and the peace and joy that a relationship with Him brings. I wanted that not just for Billy's sake but also for Douglas and Courtney's sake.

However, even though divorcing Billy was no longer an option for me, I was really not interested in getting our marriage back together. I desperately wanted a husband, just someone other than Billy—someone who was a mature, godly believer. I did not know how that would work scripturally, but I was asking anyway.

The commitment I made at that time was not to divorce Billy right then and there and not to date anyone else—even with my desire to be married to someone else. God hadn't yet moved me to the place where I was willing to say, "I'll go back to the marriage." I didn't think I could ever do that. I couldn't imagine going back to the craziness and the chaos that we had lived with. I couldn't imagine how I could ever like or love my husband again or live under the same roof or do any of the things a wife needs to do for her husband. Plus, I had told Billy that reconciliation was impossible without Jesus Christ in his life, and there was no sign that this was going to happen, Dr. Bright's prayer notwithstanding.

Having so many conflicting emotions, I wrote in my journal:

> Lord, I long for a husband to worship with, to tell the world about You with, and to be a father to Douglas and Courtney. Lord, can it be Billy? Will he come to You? O, Lord, I pray for Your intervention!

But then shortly thereafter, I wrote:

> Lord, please give me strength to follow through with a divorce.

While I wanted to do what God said in His Word, which meant not divorcing, I also had a strong desire for a godly marriage. I couldn't figure out how that could be, and I was still conflicted.

COULD I FORGIVE?

One day, a year after my time at Campus Crusade staff training, Billy called and asked if the kids and I would go to a Yankees game with him that Sunday. I answered, "If you go to church with us first." And to my great surprise, he accepted. It was a wonderful and memorable day—warm, clear, and sunny. I can even tell you what I was wearing: white shorts, a polo shirt with an orange sweater over my shoulders, and light-brown lizard flats and belt. Everyone at our church was incredibly kind; they all came over to welcome Billy. The kids, now six and eight, were all smiles. The three of us had prayed together en route to church for Daddy to hear the message and, of course, for him to come to know Jesus.

After church, the four of us drove to Yankee Stadium. I couldn't tell you who won or lost that game or even what team the Yankees played. I only know that later that evening, Billy called me to say, "I still love you, and I had a wonderful day with my family." This was definitely a turning point. It was that evening that I told the Lord, "Whatever You want to do with me is okay. If You want to keep me single and separated for the rest of my life because that is how You want to use me in the lives of others, I'm okay with that." Finally, I completely surrendered to whatever God had planned for my life and marriage.

I started to realize that through the process of praying for Billy, my heart had been softening toward him, and my anger was subsiding. I asked God to cause my heart to forgive him so that I would obey Jesus' teaching on forgiveness: "Then Peter came up and said to him [Jesus], "Lord, how often will my brother sin against me, and I forgive him? As many as seven times?" Jesus said to him, "I do not say to you seven times, but seventy-seven times" (Matt. 18:21–22). Jesus instructed Peter to forgive seventy-seven times, which we take to mean an unlimited amount of times, without keeping track! Most of me did not want to forgive Billy, partly because I did not know how to forgive the way he had hurt me so deeply. He had caused our family to fall apart; he had caused all my dreams to be dashed to pieces. He had made me feel worthless and undesirable, and he had hurt our children. How could I forgive all that?

I didn't know, so I went to the Lord in prayer and asked *Him* to cause my heart to forgive. I asked for forgiveness for not wanting to forgive, and I asked God to make the transaction in my heart because I could not. Little by little, forgiveness occurred, and I realized it when I stopped making sarcastic comments. I stopped my litany—to anyone who would listen—of all Billy's faults, and I became willing to go back to the marriage. My eyes opened to the misery and unhappiness in Billy's life, and I continued to pray for him wholeheartedly. I was truly sorry for him, and I desperately ached for him to know Jesus. I remember one time of prayer, on my knees at the altar at church several weeks later, sobbing and crying out to God to draw Billy Rose to Himself and to deliver him from the addiction and the emptiness of his life.

Knowing all that Billy had done and the lifestyle he was continuing to live, it would have been easy to give up and believe that he was beyond saving. But I knew God could do it, because Isaiah 55:8–9 says, "For my thoughts are not your thoughts, neither are your ways my ways, declares the LORD. For as the heavens are higher than the earth, so are my ways higher than your ways and my thoughts than your thoughts." I could not even imagine how God was going to bring Billy to Him, but I trusted in God's power to do anything in His way and in His time. I didn't have to figure it out. In fact, my plan would be nothing compared to God's. So I gave it over to the One who had created my husband.

Soon after that, on a Tuesday night, Billy's night to have dinner with Douglas and Courtney, we had a conversation, and I sensed he was becoming open toward God. I offered Billy a Bible, and, again to my surprise, he accepted it. Shortly after that, I received a ten-page, handwritten letter. Billy truthfully and openly shared with me that he was miserable, addicted, and praying to God for help, faith, and direction. I was ecstatic.

Not everyone, however, was pleased or excited about Billy's interested and seeking heart. One morning his mother called me at work. She blasted me for getting Billy into "this Jesus thing." I explained to her that I was not getting Billy into anything and that he was his own person making his own choices. She then said, "If he does this, I will disown and disinherit him." I calmly responded that disowning Billy was certainly a choice she could make and that I was sorry she was so upset. Shaking after I hung up the telephone, I knew the Holy Spirit had given me this gentle response. In that moment, God reminded me that although not everyone will support my faith and my obedience to Him, He will be there with me even in the difficult times.

GOD'S PROVISION

By that time it was September 1990, and we had been separated a full four years. I couldn't believe I'd spent four years as a single mom, the hardest job I could ever imagine. Children need both a mom and a dad to raise them, and I also believe parents need each other for support and sharing the load. Alone, I was constantly tired and often fighting discouragement, anger, and self-pity. I remember reading the Little House books to Courtney at bedtime. Many nights I could not get through the words because I was choking back tears of bitterness, resentment, loneliness, and exhaustion. And, while I had enough money to meet our basic needs of rent, phone, electricity, and food, there was no money for extras like movies, theater, vacations, or taxicabs. I even had to give away our dog, Homer, because, with two young children, it was impossible to walk him as often as he needed, and I no longer had the money to pay a dog walker.

About a year after I became a believer, I left my job at Macy's. My decision was based on what God said about seeking first His kingdom and His righteousness (Matt. 6:33–34) and putting my treasure in heaven (vv. 19–21). I realized that the money I was making while working wasn't all that much once I deducted what I paid a babysitter to take

care of my children, the clothes I needed for work, and the transportation to get to work. I looked at the amount that was left over and realized that maybe I could live without that income—a completely new
thought. I could be home with Douglas and Courtney and be their
mom full-time. I asked God to open the doors for me to leave my full-
time job if He willed. I told Him that I would trust Him to provide
for me. So I was able to leave my job at Macy's, and I started working
part-time at the DeMoss House. This worked perfectly, because I only
worked while the kids were in school, and I had the summers off.

I quickly began to see God in the role of provider. While I'd been
praying about leaving Macy's, I'd also asked God to bring a student to
live with us who could help out with the children in exchange for hous-
ing and a small salary. God answered this prayer with no effort at all
on my part: a young woman moved to New York City from Lincoln,
Nebraska, to work at the DeMoss House, and she needed a place to
live. So she moved into our spare eight-by-eight-foot room, helped out
with the kids, and even paid rent. God answered my prayer in the best
possible way.

God also provided through my father, who had a country home in
Upstate New York at Gipsy Trail. Many weekends Dad and my stepmother, Bobbie, would loan us their car, and I was able to escape the
city's cold, cement drudgery for a weekend in the country. For New
Yorkers, a weekend out is a wonderful refuge from the intense lifestyle
in the city. The summer after I began work at the DeMoss House, I
sublet our apartment to a friend in exchange for the use of her car so
that the kids and I could go to Gipsy Trail for the summer. Her car died
midway through the summer, so the next summer I put a sign on the
bulletin board at Bible study, and other friends offered the use of their
station wagon, fondly called "Heapster." I sublet the apartment, and we
were off to the country again.

During those summers, Douglas and Courtney went to day camp
from 9:00 a.m. until 2:00 p.m. Instead of playing ladies tennis, I seized
this time to read my Bible and to take long bike rides through the hilly

countryside, listening to taped sermons. My batteries, both physical and spiritual, were refueled through these wonderful times at Gipsy Trail, and I was so grateful to God and to my dad for their provision.

The Lord also provided for me through strangers. One Sunday on the way home from church, while running to catch the crosstown bus, a man dressed as a clown approached us and gave us three tickets to the Big Apple Circus. Walking into the big tent, we knew God had provided this afternoon treat for us. I was carrying two large china platters that had been used at church for a wedding the day before, but that didn't matter. And God provided over and over. Friends from church took Douglas and Courtney for afternoon outings. Another friend gave me all her children's outgrown clothes. The days she would drop off boxes were like Christmas. Douglas, Courtney, and I were so grateful, and I was learning that God blesses obedience and takes care of every need.

Yet God wasn't done showing me how He is my provider. My sister, Heidi, and her husband, Bob, took Douglas and Courtney to their summer cottage near the beach for a weekend. I believe that the greatest gift you can give a single mom is to take her kids out and do something with them to give her an afternoon, evening, or weekend off. When you're a single parent, you're on 24/7/365. Because there was no break, offers from friends or family to give me even a tiny break from the constant demands were amazing.

I'll never forget walking with my pastor's wife one day. There were some beautiful plants sitting outside of a store, and I said, "Oh, look how beautiful they are!" So she went and bought me one. It was at a time when I certainly didn't have any extra spending money for anything like that. She didn't either, but she bought it anyway. It flattened me to the ground that she would do that. That incident opened my eyes to a whole different way of living and giving to people who need to know someone cares.

God also provided me with a prayer partner. When I first started going to Bible study, a woman named Vicky Todd said, "Let's be prayer partners." I had no idea what that meant, but I agreed. So every once in a while she would call me, and we would talk about what was going on in our lives and then pray together. We often prayed about Billy, and she talked a lot about reconciliation. She told me how much Billy loved me, and she encouraged me not to give up. Vicky also came over to the house to help out. She loved Douglas and Courtney and would read stories and sing songs to them. She was a godsend and a true friend and unlike any other friend I'd ever had. She even babysat the kids one entire weekend so I could have my first vacation in four years—a trip to a generous friend's condo in Naples, Florida, using airline mileage accrued while at Macy's. God provided the friend, her heart to help, and a time away for a very weary mom.

I was so grateful, and I had never been truly grateful before for anything. In the past, no matter what I had—a lovely home, beautiful clothes, a husband—it was never enough. I really did not appreciate anything. I was totally consumed with worry about what others thought about me, my children, what we did, how we dressed, and whom we knew. But God was truly changing me and delivering me from my empty way of life. That gave me great joy during this time. The love and generosity that my friend Vicky and others showed was a huge part of God's bringing me to trust Him, as I saw Him express His love through His people.

Chapter 9

REUNITED

WHILE GOD WAS OBVIOUSLY PROVIDING in a physical sense, He also provided amazingly when it came to reaching Billy with the gospel. I was cohosting a house church with another couple, Dave and Becky Swanson. Dave's dad was head of an organization called Baseball Chapel, and he came to the house church one night and gave me a Baseball Chapel newsletter with Bobby Richardson's picture on the front. That name was familiar to me: I remembered Billy talking about his childhood hero, Bobby Richardson, who had played for the New York Yankees. Wearing number one, he'd batted first and played second base. Billy, while captain of his prep-school baseball team, had also batted first and played second base while wearing number one. I shared this information with Dave, and I asked him if there was any way to have Billy and Bobby meet. In September 1990, Dave sent me two tickets to a Baseball Chapel Hall of Fame luncheon at the Downtown Athletic Club, which was located just a few blocks from the Sporting Club. I invited Billy, and he accepted my invitation. Bobby was not only at the luncheon but was also the keynote speaker, and we were seated with him. Afterward he went back to the Sporting Club with Billy and spent the afternoon telling Billy about his faith and his God. He gave Billy *The Bobby Richardson Story*, his book about his life, faith, and baseball career.[7]

Unbeknownst to me, Billy was starting to realize that there had to be more to life than what he was experiencing with his drugs, sex, and rock-and-roll lifestyle at the Sporting Club. So he began watching a televangelist on Sunday mornings. He would get down on his knees, praying and crying. He didn't know to whom he was praying, but pray he did. During that time he also read Bobby's book, which I was shocked to learn because Billy is not a reader. Then in December he accepted an invitation to an outreach Christmas dinner hosted by Nancy DeMoss at her home in New York City.

While I was working at the DeMoss House, we would go through the comment cards when the dinner was finished. That evening we found Billy's card, and we saw that he checked the top box, which said, "I prayed to receive Jesus Christ as my Lord and Savior tonight." I was sitting there with Nancy DeMoss and several other people, and we rejoiced and immediately began to pray. I arrived home, and my phone rang. It was Billy, and he said, "Thank you very much. I just want you to know, I checked the box." And he hung up.

Then the strangest thing happened. I received a phone call from a man who was looking for my husband. He was yelling and using terrible language on the phone, claiming that Billy was stealing his girlfriend. Immediately, I knew that the enemy was trying to take away that amazing joy over what had happened that night—which he couldn't. I didn't even call Billy to challenge him about what I'd heard the man say; it was just too obvious that Satan was after us. But the good news is, once a person prays to receive Christ, he is *in Christ*.

Billy knew that accepting Christ wasn't the only change he needed to make. There was still the cocaine habit to take care of. So six weeks later he entered Gracie Square Hospital's drug rehab program. During the first night, he went through horrendous withdrawals, so he got down on his knees and cried out to the Lord. Almost instantaneously, the withdrawal symptoms vanished. The nauseous feeling that he had felt for years just left him. He felt a peace and a calm, which filled and surrounded him, that he had never experienced before. He told the floor counselor, "I'm good. I can go home now." At the floor counselor's insistence (and unbelief), Billy stayed a full week. At the end of the week, he checked out of rehab and returned to work in the lions' den—the Sporting Club. However, God gave him the ability to resist the drugs, and he has not touched cocaine again to this day.

HOMECOMING

In some ways, the time after Billy became a believer was the hardest of all for me. I thought, *He's saved. He's sober. So why isn't he coming home?* During his time in rehab, I constantly prayed for Billy with the children, my friends, and my coworkers. He called me every few hours, talking and crying. By the time he finished rehab, my expectations had become unrealistic, and I was exhausted. When he didn't move back home immediately, I was shocked and a little angry.

The Lord provided for me once again in the form of BJ and Sheila Weber. BJ came to preach at our church one Sunday in April 1991 after the rector had moved away. I had met BJ and Sheila briefly at a DeMoss House Christmas party, and BJ had been at the Baseball Chapel luncheon that Billy and I had attended. I had heard that BJ "worked with difficult cases." That was definitely us! I leaned over to Billy during the sermon and whispered, "I think he'd counsel us." And Billy answered, "I'd talk to him." At the time I was completely unaware that BJ was the chaplain for the New York Yankees.

Although I had known the Lord for three years, and Billy was now a believer too, we had so many issues to overcome. Both of us were selfish, judgmental, not very good at communicating, and had type-A personalities. We desperately needed guidance and direction. We had been raised in completely different ways and each had our own view of what marriage should be. BJ led us through *His Needs, Her Needs*, Willard F. Harley's book on marriage.[8] The revelations were numerous for us both.

I would walk down the street and see other happy families and wish I was married to one of the men I saw, at times thinking once again that another marriage partner was the answer. Billy's struggle involved other women. BJ called each of us to account in these and other areas. It was hard work, very emotional, and there were many times we were both tempted to simply call it quits.

One night in early October 1991, BJ and Sheila came over to my apartment to have dinner with Billy and me. Once the children had gone to bed, we sat around the dining room table and tackled some of our issues. Billy was still not interested in coming home. He was happy to spend time with his family and take me on dates, but he did not want to move home and take responsibility for his family. I was having a hard time understanding his reticence, and my patience was wearing thin. Sheila suggested to Billy that he needed to make a decision; he could no longer go on being single at whim and then have his family there when he wanted it. She said, "You can't have your cake and eat it too! You need to decide if you want to be single or married, and then make the commitment." I was thankful that Sheila stated the truth so clearly. Billy was so furious that he walked out of the apartment, claiming we were all pushing him too hard.

The more Billy delayed, the more I sought the Lord. I was frustrated, yet I was becoming aware of the fact that I could not control Billy, that I wasn't meant to control him, that God was sovereign and in charge, and that I needed to trust Him. I had a vague understanding that God had to be the one motivating Billy to come home, and I began to let go of the situation and live as best as I could in this predicament: married, not living together, and not really sure about the future. But God knew, and He was sure about what the future would hold, and that became enough. He became my refuge.

Douglas and Courtney struggled too. "Is Daddy coming home? Will Daddy live here again? Why hasn't he come home?" My answer to them was, "Our hope is in the Lord."

During this time, Billy's mother was diagnosed with leukemia. Her health deteriorated rapidly, and she was hospitalized two times. One particular day, while visiting her in the hospital, she apologized for giving me a hard time about Billy and Jesus, and she thanked me for this new and sober direction her son's life was taking. Then, on December 10, 1991, she had a seizure and entered Lenox Hill Hospital. Billy called me at work and asked me to meet him at the hospital. After getting his mom situated in the intensive care unit, as we were leaving the hospital he turned to me and said, "I'm going to my apartment to pack my bags. I'm coming home."

And so, on December 10, 1991, Billy Rose moved back into our apartment. We had been separated for five and a half years. My journal entry read:

December 11, 1991

Billy is home, after five and a half years. His heart is breaking as his mother lays dying. My heart aches for him and trusts You, oh Lord, as You bring us together in these circumstances. We are at peace with each other. I had envisioned great fanfare for our reunion—a ceremony, a honeymoon, "Welcome Home, Daddy" signs everywhere. Yet You, oh Lord, know that would set us up for unattainable expectations. Instead, Lord, Your plan is so much wiser. Billy packed up this morning, came over, and unpacked. Douglas and Courtney came home from school: "Daddy is home!" They were amazed. Before they arrived, Billy, in tears, asked me to pray for us. We exalt You, oh Lord!

We celebrated Courtney's seventh birthday one week later as a whole family. We went to see *Peter Pan* on Broadway, a night we all remember vividly. Courtney said to me that night, "You know, Mommy, God can do anything. If He could bring Daddy home, which was never going to happen, He can do anything!"

On December 21, 1991, three days later, Billy's seventy-two-year-old mother, Bernice Levinson Rose, died. We buried his mom at the family cemetery on Long Island with BJ there to support us. Billy shared his new faith at her small family-only funeral.

That January, Douglas wrote a paper for his English class that was subsequently published in the school's literary magazine. The title was "The Best Day Ever." The paper was about a young boy who came home from school one afternoon to find the front hall filled with suitcases. His daddy was home after being gone for five and a half years.

STILL MUCH TO LEARN

Once Billy came home, the real work began. Daily life—the day-in, day-out daily routine—was hard to get used to. We had both been essentially single for several years, and I, for one, was not quite ready for the changes that Billy brought to our household. I hadn't let the children watch TV on school nights, but Billy enjoyed watching sports every night. He even temporarily stacked two TVs in our living room so he could watch two things at once. I was also fairly strict about what the children could eat. For instance, I didn't let them eat sugary cereal, but Billy bought Trix and Cocoa Puffs. Things were definitely changing!

We both had so much to learn. I was still angry, thought I was god-lier than Billy, and acted horribly "holier than thou." Yes, I was happy Billy was home, but I wasn't at peace with many of his choices. We still owned the Sporting Club, which I saw as a source of many of our problems. I wanted Billy to live the way I wanted him to live and to make choices I wanted, such as selling the restaurant. I did not fully understand the biblical formula for submission or marriage. My expectations were high and unrealistic; they consisted of instant maturity in the Lord and a happy, biblical marriage. During the previous year I had read many Christian books on marriage, and I knew we were far from what was described, which was tremendously discouraging to me. Nobody explained that biblical marriage doesn't happen overnight—even for longtime believers. I thought it should just automatically happen when both spouses are following the Lord.

I was fearful that if I didn't make Billy happy and meet all his needs, he'd leave. But at the same time, I was so frustrated that the man I had married wasn't meeting my expectations, and I still harbored thoughts about being married to a godly, spiritual leader. Billy was not yet that man, and I wasn't sure he would ever be. Yet I had promised and covenanted before God fifteen years earlier to take Billy as my wedded husband, in plenty and want, in joy and sorrow, in sickness and health. I knew that a marriage contract is a covenant between a man and a woman before God forever. I had to continually take myself to Malachi 2:14–15, where God laments broken marriage:

> But you say, "Why does he not?" Because the LORD was witness between you and the wife of your youth, to whom you have been faithless, though she is your companion and your wife by covenant. Did he not make them one, with a portion of the Spirit in their union? And what was the one God seeking? Godly offspring. So guard yourselves in your spirit, and let none of you be faithless to the wife of your youth.

I would also turn to Proverbs 2:16–17, where we are told about the "Forbidden woman . . . who forsakes the companion of her youth and forgets the covenant of her God." I knew I was bound to Bill Rose. I also knew that I did not want to be the "wayward wife" described in the proverb but instead wanted to be a God-honoring wife, keeping the promise I had made at our wedding ceremony. And I knew I wanted our offspring to be godly! We had experienced plenty of sorrow, and I was now ready and waiting for the advantages of this covenant. I was waiting on God, whom I knew could and would deliver on the many promises He had made to me through His Word over the previous years:

- "But seek first the kingdom of God and his righteousness, and all these things will be added to you" (Matt. 6:33).

- "Delight yourself in the LORD, and he will give you the desires of your heart" (Ps. 37:4).
- "Trust in the LORD with all your heart, and do not lean on your own understanding. In all your ways acknowledge him, and he will make straight your paths" (Prov. 3:5–6).
- "And all these blessings shall come upon you and overtake you, if you obey the voice of the LORD your God" (Deut. 28:2).
- "Bring the full tithe into the storehouse... put me to the test, says the LORD of hosts, if I will not open the windows of heaven for you and pour down for you a blessing until there is no more need" (Mal. 3:10).
- "For I know the plans I have for you, declares the LORD, plans for welfare and not for evil, to give you a future and a hope" (Jer. 29:11).

Through these verses in the Old and New Testaments, God gave me promises to cling to through this trying time of reconciliation: promises of blessing, hope, fulfilled desires, and a straight path in life. I knew our reconciliation was from God and was a blessing, but we had far to go to achieve a true biblical marriage. My journal entry one year after Billy was home illustrates our struggle:

December 20, 1992

> Lord, I am struggling with so many memories and feelings of being alone. Billy is still around so little (working so many hours at the Sporting Club, including Saturdays and Sundays), and I have been spending weekends alone with the children for ten years. These issues hurt. Douglas and Courtney need a dad to play with, and I need Billy on the weekends to be a part of the family activities. Lord, please plant forgiveness in my heart; please give me the ability to let things go. Please show me how to raise my children in these circumstances.

Despite our many issues, we both persevered. Did I believe that God could bring healing to each of us individually and to the marriage relationship? This was the bottom line of what we faced. Some days the problems between us seemed insurmountable.

At other times it was clear that God was at work, and we had hope. So we chose to go forward, believing that God would make our path straight, that He would bless us if we obeyed Him, and that His plans for us were good and would give us hope and a future. We chose to go forward, however imperfectly, with El Shaddai, the all-sufficient God and the witness to the covenant we had made to each other before Him fifteen years earlier.

Chapter 10

OVERCOMING EXPECTATIONS

SOON AFTER BECOMING A BELIEVER, I began to read the Bible every day. When I did, the emptiness that I had tried to fill with people and things started to fill up with the Lord. My desire for other things began to fade. I truly saw the Bible as God's love letter to me—His way of telling me who He is, what He requires of me, how much He loves me, and so much more. My desire for God and His Word became an insatiable hunger.

I also started another habit that I continue to this day—reading through the entire Bible each year, using a one-year Bible. I was so excited to come to God's Word every morning and see what He was going to teach me. As I read through His Word, He started changing my perspective from "Vicki is most important" to "God is most important." I was so enthralled by God and all He did for His chosen people—the Israelites, the Jewish people, of which I am one. I had hope and joy for the first time in years because, as God says in Psalm 19:7–8, "The law of the LORD is perfect, reviving the soul . . . the precepts of the LORD are right, rejoicing the heart." His Word was reviving my soul and giving joy to my heart. I loved learning about God's Word during my daily quiet time, in my Bible study, and during Sunday morning services. I just couldn't get enough, and that desire didn't lessen as time went on.

God then gave me the opportunity to take my Bible study to the next level—leading a small group in Bible Study Fellowship (BSF). BSF is an in-depth, interdenominational Bible study that helps people know God and further equips them to effectively serve the church throughout the world. BSF classes meet all over the world, both in the evenings and during the day. My friend Myrna Anderson had started the first Manhattan BSF class. It was a night class, and she wanted to start a day class for women like me who were busy with children and family matters at night but could attend BSF during the day. When Billy moved back home, he requested I resign from my job since our work schedules were so different and because he was again financially supporting our family. So I joined Myrna and a group of other women to pray together and subsequently launch a pilot daytime BSF class. I was a discussion leader in that first class, and I later moved into the core leadership group of BSF's New York City day class as administrator.

In the meantime, we were learning to live together as a family again. The kids were ecstatic that Daddy was home, and Billy began spending more time with us than he had before the separation. He still spent many hours at the Sporting Club, but he also became more involved in our family life and in parenting, which had not interested him before. He would go to parents' nights at school, he attended Douglas's and Courtney's sporting events, and he would sometimes take them to the restaurant on Saturday mornings to hang out with him and watch cartoons on the big screen. He insisted we find a church where we would be spiritually challenged, so we found a new church, but he still spent many Sunday mornings at the Sporting Club.

Looking back, I can see that he did put in more effort than he had before the separation, but at the time I was not satisfied. Billy still wasn't fulfilling my expectations. I wanted him to be a godly husband overnight, and he wasn't. Then again, I hadn't necessarily become a godly wife overnight either, but from my perspective, I was working a lot harder at it than he was. After all, I was spending much time in prayer and in God's Word, I faithfully attended church, and I held a leadership position in BSF.

What I didn't realize was that we were two different people with two very different paths as believers. Billy wasn't progressing as a believer in the same ways I was, and God wasn't doing exactly the same things in Billy as He was doing in me in the same time frame, and that made me frustrated. From almost the moment I became a Christian, I held firm convictions about what was right and wrong; I saw things as black-and-white. I also had an almost overwhelming desire to know as much as I could about the Lord. That wasn't the way God planned things for Billy, and I couldn't understand it. I thought that he should desire the same things that I did, both for his spiritual life and for our family. I thought I was right and he was wrong on most issues. And because of the things he had done, I really didn't trust Billy or his ideas. I blamed Billy for my unhappiness instead of seeking God for contentment, and I was not always patient with him. This kind of thinking does *not* enhance a marriage in any way and certainly didn't serve us well, but with God's help we didn't give up.

THE SIMPLE—AND DIFFICULT—TRUTH

To any reader who finds herself in the same situation I was in, I want to encourage you to do the following: seek God, bathe yourself in His Word, hold fast to His promises, and pray according to His will. That's the nutshell, and it looks like a simple list of things to do, but you and I both know that while it might be simple in concept, it is often difficult in execution! In order for any of that to be effective, we have to first get past ourselves and realize that God is in control and then relinquish our desire for control. Again, that's simple but not easy.

In my situation, I was not satisfied with how things were progressing, and I had to remind myself to "But seek first the kingdom of God and his righteousness, and all these things will be added to you" (Matt. 6:33). In other words, if I would seek God first, instead of just barreling ahead on my own terms and insisting that God make Billy behave a certain way, God would take care of the details. Therefore, I could rest in God doing what needed to be done. This is called "surrender."

I continued to have high expectations, which meant I was still comparing Billy to others (including myself) and wanted my own way. I was anxious that I wouldn't get what I wanted, either from Billy or the marriage. Philippians 4:6–8 addressed this situation for me, and as I memorized it, I began to put it into practice.

> Do not be anxious about anything, but in everything by prayer and supplication with thanksgiving let your requests be made known to God. And the peace of God, which surpasses all understanding, will guard your hearts and your minds in Christ Jesus. Finally, brothers, whatever is true, whatever is honorable, whatever is just, whatever is pure, whatever is lovely, whatever is commendable, if there is any excellence, if there is anything worthy of praise, think about these things. (Phil. 4:6–8)

First, I had to give my anxiety about my situation to God. Then I had to present my requests to Him—but what I had to learn to do was to present them according to His will, not Vicki's will. I definitely had an idea of how I wanted things to go for Billy and for our marriage and family, but I had to let go of my expectations under the realization that God knows what we need far better than we do. When I did this (and it took a while), God began to bring peace, and He also helped me to think about the true and noble and admirable things about my husband rather than the negatives.

God also led me to Philippians 2:14–15 to begin to help me deal with my discontent: "Do all things without grumbling or disputing, that you may be blameless and innocent, children of God without blemish in the midst of a crooked and twisted generation, among whom you shine as lights in the world." Complaining never glorifies God, and it keeps us from shining like stars. Look what complaining did for the Israelites after they escaped Egypt: it cost them forty years of desert wandering and kept them out of the Promised Land (see Num. 13–14). In other words, complaining completely ruins our witness and testimony. Complaining is a terrible habit, becomes a negative way of life, and strips away gratitude and any hope for contentment. It tells God: "I don't like what You've given me, and I don't trust You." Additionally, complaining is wearisome to our mates and completely undermines them.

Then my anger had to be dealt with. James 1:19–20 says, "Know this, my beloved brothers: let every person be quick to hear, slow to speak, slow to anger; for the anger of man does not produce the righteousness of God." One day I said to my prayer partner, "Billy makes me so angry!" She responded, lovingly and truthfully, "Vicki, Billy does not make you angry. You are an angry person." I immediately knew she was right. That's when I memorized James 1:19–20 and asked God to remove my anger. The twelve-step slogans really helped me in this area. I would stop and ask myself, "How important is it?" or, concerning a past issue, "Let the past be the past." God's Word and Spirit, along with the twelve-step tools, proved to be a winning combination over this character defect. Practicing these tools is not a onetime act; it often needs revisiting. I frequently say to myself, "How important is this, Vicki?" and, "Vicki, your anger will not bring about the righteous life that Christ desires!"

Most of all, I was impatient with Billy *and* with God. At that point in our reconciliation, I didn't realize that it takes time. Philippians 4:19 has helped me to be patient with the process: "And my God will supply every need of yours according to his riches in glory in Christ Jesus." How incredible that God promises to meet *all* of my needs and yours, too.

In the midst of all of this, God also reminded me that when I ask, He forgives all this sin in my life. First John 1:9 says, "If we confess our sins, he is faithful and just to forgive us our sins and to cleanse us from all unrighteousness." Asking God's forgiveness for all my discontent was key, and I had to keep asking daily. When I accepted Christ, all my sins—past, present, and future—were forgiven. But 1 John 1:9 tells me that I also need to repent daily of each day's sins, and when I ask God for forgiveness, the fellowship with God that sin breaks is restored. It is awesome to have this daily reminder of the work Christ did for me on the cross. He *died* so that I could be forgiven. He conquered death and rose again so that I could have eternal life. God, let me never forget this amazing truth.

GOD-HONORING PRAYER

The key in all this was (and still is) to get my eyes off my husband and onto God. I needed to look at my part and work on that, asking God to change me and to show me how to pray for my husband—not try to change him. I once heard Barbara Rainey (cofounder with her husband, Dennis Rainey, of FamilyLife, an international ministry focused on families and marriages) share on the *Revive Our Hearts* radio program that in the beginning of her marriage to Dennis, she made a list of all the negatives in Dennis and began to pray daily for God to change those things. After a very short time, she realized this was making her miserable and causing her to look only at Dennis's negatives and was not beneficial to her or to their marriage. She threw out the list, never to look at it again.

Negative and critical thinking about my husband was a huge area that I needed to work on in those early days as a believer. This critical spirit still rears its ugly head frequently and needs constant repentance. At the beginning of our reconciliation, I didn't understand all these things. It has taken time. God rarely changes us overnight, so I encourage you to be patient with the process—patient with God, your spouse, and yourself.

One book that has really helped me to pray for Billy in a God-honoring way is *Praying God's Will for My Husband,* by Lee Roberts.[9] It contains Scriptures divided by categories, such as confidence, forgiveness, obedience, and waiting on God. Praying God's Word for our husbands is the most powerful tool we have and the greatest privilege.

When we pray God's Word, we are praying according to His will, and 1 John 5:14–15 tells us: "And this is the confidence that we have toward him, that if we ask anything according to his will he hears us. And if we know that he hears us in whatever we ask, we know that we have the requests that we have asked of him." We can have confidence in approaching God. In the original Greek language, the word for "confidence" is *parresia*. It's a "freedom in speaking all that one thinks, confidence or boldness, and manifests itself in confident praying."[10] It means I can come to Him without fearing that He doesn't hear me and won't answer me. Merriam-Webster's dictionary defines confidence as "the faith or belief that one will act in a right, proper, or effective way."[11] This excites me because I know God can and will act only in the right way. He is God, and He is good and cannot do any evil. This verse teaches me that I *know* that God both hears and answers my prayer. This is key for my walk with God and for my marriage, and it enables me to stop trying to change Billy and to leave him in God's trustworthy hands.

I am grateful that God constantly reminds me that His prescriptions for our troubles and for how to pray are outlined in His Word. I can say with certainty that as you seek the Lord first in your own trials, He will also lead you to places in His Word that will speak to you and bring life to you, your spouse, and your marriage. You *can't* go wrong when you turn to God's Word.

Chapter 11

THE MARRIAGE BATTLE

AS I MENTIONED EARLIER, SOON AFTER Billy came home, we began a hunt for a new church we could attend as a family. The church I had been attending felt like home to me, and the other members had become like family. However, the pastor whom I loved so dearly had recently left, and the interim pastor didn't teach the Bible. Billy, as a brand-new Christian, wasn't satisfied with that. He told me that if he was going to go to church, he wanted to hear an inspiring and challenging biblical message. At the time, there were only a handful of evangelical churches in New York City, so our choices were limited. We tried a couple of places, and we eventually settled down at Trinity Baptist Church, which remains our church home in New York City twenty-two years later. My husband made a great choice.

Due to still owning and running the restaurant, Billy didn't always go to church, even once we found one he liked. So I kept trying to find ways to get him involved in something else that would enhance his spiritual life. In 1995 I had my chance, when some friends urged us to attend the Pro Athletes Outreach Conference. PAO is a ministry that serves Christian professional athletes and their spouses. The organization's mission is to grow these couples as disciples of Jesus so they can positively impact lives in their spheres of influence.

As part owners of the Yankees, Billy and I were part of the pro-athlete community, and we heard about the annual PAO conference from our friends John and Michele Wetteland. John was the Yankees closing pitcher and 1996 World Series Most Valuable Player (MVP), and Billy and I had come to know him and Michele. At dinner one night, Michele told Billy and me that we must go to the PAO conference. She said it would grow us both in the Lord and strengthen our marriage. I desperately wanted to go because I wanted the opportunity to learn more about God alongside my husband, but Billy was somewhat resistant. So I began to pray, asking God to somehow get us to the conference.

Billy finally reluctantly agreed to attend half of the five-day conference. However, one week before it began, his right knee gave out and became very swollen. He had already had five surgeries on the knee since his baseball-career-ending injury in high school, so he always had problems with it, but it was now in even worse shape. Billy was in great pain and was sure we would not be able to make it to Orlando to the conference. Since I had never had knee problems, I had no idea how much pain he was really in (and sympathy was not my strong point), so I kept pushing him to attend the conference. At the time I would have said that I made Billy go, but looking back, I know it was God who got us there, crutches and all. Satan was working overtime to try to keep us from going to that event, and God wasn't going to allow us to stay home, because He knew how that conference would change our lives in many ways.

When Billy and I arrived at the conference hotel, the first people we saw were Sterling and Carrey Hitchcock. Sterling was a starting pitcher for the Yankees, and he and his wife were the *only* people we knew at the conference, as the Wettelands were unable to attend due to the impending birth of their twin girls. We didn't know the Hitchcocks very well, but it was a great gift from God to see familiar Yankee faces. From our time together at that first PAO conference, a friendship developed and has grown over the years. The Hitchcocks have become like family to Billy and me and our two kids.

One of the keynote speakers at the conference, Tom Shrader, was God's healing instrument for me and our marriage. In his talk, "There Is No Off-Season," he taught that all of our lives are about God. He explained that God can use all of the circumstances of our lives—good or bad, encouraging or hurtful relationships, and even abuse or childhood trauma—to draw us closer to Him. Closeness to God is to be desired above all else, as God is the very best answer for our every need. During his talk, Tom asked everyone who had been under the age of twenty-one when one of their parents died to stand. He asked groups of people to gather around those of us who had experienced what he called "one of life's biggest traumas." As I stood, tears were streaming down my face as people I didn't know were praying for me. Billy also stood next to me, weeping and praying for me along with the others.

I had been deeply wounded by my mother's death when I was eighteen, but nobody had ever acknowledged that I had experienced one of life's greatest traumas. That night in Orlando, my wound was further opened and acknowledged, and a deep healing took place inside me. My experience that night also led to a new area of oneness with my husband. Billy came to a new understanding about this major event in my life, and he realized a connection between us due to the fact that he had recently lost his own mother.

The next afternoon during some free time, Billy and I wandered into the mall attached to the hotel, Billy still hobbling on crutches. We passed a jewelry store, and Billy led me inside. He said, "Let's buy a wedding ring for me. I want the world to know I am married to you and that I am taken and unavailable to anyone else." I was ecstatic. This was another huge answer to prayer about a long-held desire and a request I had presented to my husband on several occasions. I was jumping for joy on the inside as we chose a ring that signified my husband's desire to please me and further submit himself to our marriage.

If all of that wasn't enough to view the conference as an extraordinary success for the Rose family, it is also where I met my kindred spirit, prayer partner, and mentor, Jackie Kendall. Before going to the conference, Michele Wetteland had told me I had to meet her friend Jackie, who would be speaking at the conference. So the first thing I did after we registered was to look for and say hello to Jackie. When I found her, about seven women surrounded her, so I knew we wouldn't be able to have much of a conversation. However, I approached her, introduced myself, and then went on my way. Our paths crossed two or three other times at the conference, and I was both touched and intrigued by her teaching.

Jackie and I didn't really get to know each other at that conference, but God was working to put us together. The following summer, Jackie's family came to New York City to visit the Wettelands. Michele made me a part of their trip by asking me to take them on a tour of New York City, which included the Metropolitan Museum of Art and Central Park. I also attended the Bible studies the Kendalls led with the Yankee players and their wives that week. My time with Jackie during her week in New York served to solidify a new and obviously God-given friendship.

Billy was also taken with Jackie and her wisdom in the ways of the Lord, as he too had attended the couples Bible study the Kendalls led for some Yankee-player couples at Yankee Stadium. We would often call her to ask for advice and help with our parenting skills. Imagine— my husband wanted to know how God wanted him to parent! It was beyond my wildest dreams. When we attended that first PAO conference, we truly had no idea of the amazing ways God was going to work in our lives, and He was nowhere near to being finished.

A BATTLE FOR MARRIAGE

In those early years after Billy and I reconciled, I felt that I was in a constant spiritual battle. As a result, I quickly learned to pray in earnest. God's Word says, "And when they prevailed . . . for they cried out to God in the battle, and he granted their urgent plea because they trusted in him" (1 Chron. 5:20). Billy and I were in a battle to survive and to live victoriously in Christ. In fact, we are still in a battle today for our marriage, though it is a different kind of battle now that we are more mature in the Lord and are committed to Him and to our marriage. We fight to keep our marriage strong and to keep Satan from trying to destroy it.

Regardless of the kind of battle you are facing in your marriage, I want to encourage you to pray—pray about every single detail of your situation and then pray some more. It's what God's Word prescribes for us. First Thessalonians 5:16–18 says, "Rejoice always, pray without ceasing, give thanks in all circumstances; for this is the will of God in Christ Jesus for you." There are some heavy commands in those few short verses.

I don't know about you, but always being joyful does not come easily for me. When things are going great, sure, I can be joyful. But when trials come, I have to constantly ask God to let His joy be my strength (Neh. 8:10). We can't will ourselves to be joyful. I have found that the second command in those verses from 1 Thessalonians is what makes the first one possible: "pray without ceasing," or continually.

But is it even possible to pray continually? The way I see it, that command doesn't stand alone. It should be taken in combination with the next one: "give thanks in all circumstances." As I walk through my day, I thank God for everything. I thank Him for sunshine; I thank Him for rain. I thank Him for my breakfast, lunch, and dinner. I thank Him for my car and for the New York City subway system. I thank Him for arms and legs that allow me to clean my house and make my bed. When my plans go as intended or when they run amok, I give thanks. In the process of thanking God for everything in all circumstances, I find that I am constantly talking to Him. And, as I thank God for everything, I find that my attitude has changed, and I am, in fact, joyful. Try it yourself, and see if it doesn't work for you, too.

If you are in the trenches for your marriage, I also want to encourage you to spend time with God in prayer and in His Word *every* morning. There is no better way to begin your day, and there is no other way to know God and to be able to trust and surrender to Him than by communicating with Him and knowing His Word. There is also great power in praying God's Word back to Him as you read it each day. God's Word helps us remember who He is—Almighty Lord, all-powerful, all-knowing, the Creator, Redeemer, Sustainer, victorious one. I daily thank God that He is all of those things (and so much more) and remind myself how great He is. I praise Him for all His wondrous works, using a psalm such as Psalm 145. So many mornings I awaken with fear and dread of the day ahead and the issues in my life. After a time of praising God, these thoughts are replaced by hope and joy in a supernatural exchange. My negative thoughts are replaced by God's greatness. I often repeat this process throughout the day when I find myself struggling again.

After thanking and praising God, I ask Him to show me my sins, forgive them (Ps. 51:10), and deliver me from habitual sins. Remember, 1 John 1:9 assures us that when we ask God to forgive us, we are completely forgiven. Knowing I am completely forgiven brings joy and gratitude to my heart, regardless of my circumstances, and I believe it can do the same for you.

I then present God with my requests for family, friends, and others who have asked for prayer. Sometimes I pray for a long time, and other times the prayers are short. But I find that praying for others helps me to take the focus off of me, and it relieves me of the burden of trying to (or believing that I can) fix other people or their problems on my own.

During my morning prayers, I am completely honest with God about everything. I tell Him what I can bear and what I can't bear and need relief from. When I was a single mom, for instance, I often asked God to bring me some relief with child care, and someone would call me out of the blue and ask if they could take the kids for an afternoon. God does answer prayer, and He blesses our honesty and vulnerability.

I know that many of you are thinking that you just don't have time to read God's Word and pray like this every day. You have kids and husbands and jobs and a million things to do. I've been there; I know what it's like. But I also know that it is possible to spend time with the Lord every single day, especially when motivated by Scriptures such as, "But seek first the kingdom of God and his righteousness" (Matt. 6:33); "This Book of the Law shall not depart from your mouth, but you shall meditate on it day and night"(Josh. 1:8); and, "Oh how I love your law! It is my meditation all the day" (Ps. 119:97).

During my separation, there was often seemingly no time to spare. However, I asked God to awaken me before the children awoke so that I would have time alone with Him. I realized that prioritizing God's Word actually gave me more time in my day by giving me peace and eliminating worry and anxiety. During those early mornings, I asked God for Billy's salvation, for my heart to be changed and to forgive Billy, and eventually for our marriage to be restored and for oneness in our marriage. In that time, God drew near to me and allowed me to know Him in a much deeper way. Psalm 145:18 says, "The Lord is near to all who call on him, to all who call on him in truth," and James 4:8 tells us, "Come near to God and he will come near to you." God cannot resist coming near to those who call out to Him.

As we discussed in the last chapter, we have confidence that when we pray according to God's will, He *will* hear us (1 John 5:14). As I bring my requests to Him in my battle for my marriage, I know that He hears my prayers. I also know that if I am praying according to His will, I will receive what I have asked for. This brings me great relief, because I have handed over the reins of my life to God Almighty, the Creator of all things. When I give my problems to God and ask Him to fix them according to His will, I know He will do it. This gives me great freedom, absence of worry, and even joy, because I know He is trustworthy and that His will for my life is what I truly desire.

For those in the marriage battle, I also encourage counseling. Billy and I have invested in our marriage through much godly and biblical counseling and are now reaping the benefits. There have been times— especially at the beginning—when our sessions were difficult and painful and didn't bring the immediate results I was looking for. During those situations, I prayed about every detail, both before a session and after, and I would ask my trusted prayer partner to also lift up the situation in prayer. I encourage you to invite one or two godly and trustworthy women (not your whole Bible study) to confide in and who can pray for you.

The battle for marriage is real and fierce, and we must use every tool God has given us. In Ephesians 6:17, God tells us that the sword of the Spirit is "the word of God." Use it as your sword to battle the enemy, like Jesus did when He was tempted by Satan in the desert (Matt. 4:1–11) and trust that God is on your side and will hear your prayers, and the devil will flee.

Chapter 12

A PRAYER
IS ANSWERED

THERE ARE TIMES IN EVERY Christian's life when events and
circumstances come together in a way that can only be attributed
to God. That's not to say that God's not intimately involved in all the
details of our lives, but there are just some instances where it is abundantly clear that He is at work. What is interesting about these times is
how we can often look back and see how God was at work for years or
even decades to make everything come together just right to bless us in
unimaginable ways.

In Ephesians 3:20 Paul tells us that God "is able to do far more
abundantly than all that we ask or think, according to the power at
work within us." I have seen God do "immeasurably more" in my life. I
know it is possible and that He wants to give good things to His children. I also know that it sometimes takes a long time for it to come
about, because He is working in ways that we cannot see to bless us in
ways we don't even know we need to be blessed.

In 1997, Billy, the kids, and I moved to Florida. When I look back
on the circumstances that led to that move, it is abundantly clear that
God was at work every step of the way and was answering in ways I
never could have imagined, prayers that had been uttered years earlier.

OPEN HOUSES AND OPEN DOORS

During the years after our reconciliation, Billy often talked abstractly about living in Florida. He dreamed about living on the water and having a boat. The idea terrified me. I had never lived anywhere but New York City, with the exception of my college years, and I had no idea how to move to another state where I was not familiar with the neighborhoods or schools. On the other hand, I did like the thought of getting away from the brutal New York winters and our twelve hundred-square-foot apartment. I felt I could adjust to the changes if I could have sunshine and more space.

Billy and I had talked about and actually looked into moving elsewhere in New York City. We needed more space, and we felt we finally had the financial means to move out of our tiny apartment, but we found that the amount of money that it would cost to buy even a little bit more space in Manhattan was ludicrous. Then we started looking in the suburbs of New York, but nothing appealed to both of us. Once we seriously started talking about moving, we realized that if we left New York, Billy's dad, who was in his late nineties at the time, would be alone with no family around. We decided that we needed and wanted to stay in New York as long as he was alive.

Meanwhile, during one of my conversations with my new friend Jackie, I mentioned how we'd talked about possibly moving to Florida someday in the distant future. I told her we'd like to live in the Fort Lauderdale area, since that was the Yankees' spring training home at the time. We spent a few weeks there every spring and would attend church at Calvary Chapel. We liked the church so much that even after the Yankees moved their spring training home to Tampa, Billy and I went to Fort Lauderdale for our anniversary in February so we could attend Calvary Chapel and Billy could play golf. When I explained all of this—and my fears about moving—to Jackie, she immediately told me about her friend Cynthia, who had just moved to Fort Lauderdale. Cynthia had done a ton of research on schools and neighborhoods in Fort Lauderdale, and Jackie encouraged me to meet with her the next time she visited New York. She knew I would appreciate all the advice and tips Cynthia could give me about settling a family in this new location.

A few weeks after that conversation, Billy's dad passed away and went home to be with the Lord. Three months earlier, this one-hundred-year-old Jewish man had prayed with Billy and me and accepted Jesus Christ as his Messiah—his Savior—thus ensuring his home in heaven. We were so thankful that we had made the decision to stay in New York during his last years so that we could spend time with him and show him the way to our Savior.

Although we no longer needed to stay in New York, I still didn't think we would really move to Florida. A few weeks later, when Jackie called to tell me that her friend Cynthia would be in New York the following week, I told Jackie I was too busy to meet her. After all, I thought, what was the point in talking to someone I didn't know about a move I wasn't going to make? However, God had different plans.

Four months later Billy asked if I'd like to take a twentieth-anniversary trip to Paris, London, and Rome. I loved Europe, but I turned down the invitation. First, I was weary from New York City life, and I knew that wouldn't be a restful trip. Second, I wanted to save such a trip for a day when we'd be able to afford to take the kids along. And, finally, I also knew that if we were in Europe, I'd want to buy clothes in the fashion capitals of the world, but I didn't need any more clothes. (Can you imagine me saying that, after my *Women's Wear Daily* aspirations as a young woman? The Lord truly did change me in many ways.) So instead of going to Europe, we decided to spend some days relaxing in the sun in Fort Lauderdale, and Billy suggested we look at houses while we were there. We weren't going to look seriously. He just wanted to see what was available for what price. I agreed and made a mental note to call Jackie to get her friend's phone number so I could contact her during our trip. I didn't have to make that call, because God had already planned our meeting.

The next day I was at my Bible Study Fellowship class, and a visitor walked in and signed the guest book. She wrote down that she was from Fort Lauderdale. I told her we visited Fort Lauderdale often, and she looked at my name tag and said, "You're Jackie's friend, aren't you?" Cynthia had had no idea it was my class, and I'd had no idea she was in town. Needless to say, God knew.

Cynthia connected us with a Realtor in Fort Lauderdale, who spent a day with us on our vacation showing us homes. We apologized for wasting her time, as we weren't really interested in buying a house; we just wanted to see what was available at what price. We also told her we *definitely* were not going to build a house. We looked at houses all day, but we didn't see anything we liked. At the end of the day as we were driving back to the hotel, we passed an open-house sign. I looked at the house and liked it, so we asked the Realtor to stop. We toured the house, and after we'd walked through it, Billy and I looked at each other and said, "This is our house." In all of our house hunting in New York and earlier that day in Florida, Billy and I had never liked the same house. This wasn't surprising, as we have wildly different tastes, so when we found a house we both liked, we took it as a sign.

The next day Billy and I toured a school and fell in love with it. We knew that was where we wanted to send our kids to school, but it was a twenty-five-minute drive from the house we had found. As a mom who was used to sending her kids off to school on public transportation in New York City, the thought of spending at least two hours a day in the car taking my kids to and from school was overwhelming. I just didn't think I could do it.

We looked at houses near the school for several days. We didn't find any we liked, so we talked to the builder of "our house," and discovered that he could build that exact same house in a different location. We walked onto a piece of property just two miles from the school, and Billy said, "This is it. This is where we're supposed to be." The property was actually two lots being sold together, and we just wanted one lot, so we only made an offer on one. The owner didn't even respond to the offer.

We prayed about the situation, as we had done all throughout that trip, asking God that if it was His will for us to have that property at that location, He would open the doors to make it happen. If the doors didn't open, we would stay in New York. As God would have it, we discovered that the property owner was a lifelong friend of George Steinbrenner, the Yankees owner, our friend and partner. George made a phone call, and by the end of the week, we had our lot. We didn't think God could have made things any clearer that it was His will for us to move to Florida. We were convinced that this move wasn't just a whim of ours but was truly God's plan for our family.

MY SUNSHINE PRAYER

When we got home from the trip that turned our lives upside down, I couldn't help but think of the "sunshine prayer" I had uttered seven years earlier. During my separation from Billy, his parents had agreed to pay for the kids' schooling, which was an answer to prayer and a huge blessing to me, especially since his parents were not happy with my decision to follow Jesus. Courtney had been accepted into the Chapin School, the only secular school in New York City at that time where the students sang hymns, said prayers, and memorized Bible verses. I would have loved for the kids to go to a Christian school, but I knew Billy's family wouldn't support that decision.

I walked the twenty blocks (one mile) to my in-laws' house to pick up the tuition check for Courtney's school. It was an extremely cold day, but I didn't care, because God had been faithful. I was filled with joy by the way He was providing for my children and me. I walked along the East River and watched the water sparkling in the sun and into the nearby apartments.

I have always loved sunshine; it makes me feel healthy. When I was four years old, I contracted pneumonia, and the doctor suggested we go to Florida to heal and fortify my body in the sun. My parents couldn't afford a Florida vacation, so they bought a sunlamp instead. I think this is why my body has always craved sunlight, which is hard to come by in New York City apartments. In fact, the apartment where I had lived from the time Billy and I were married received only about twenty minutes of sunshine each day. I soaked up that twenty minutes every chance I had.

So as I walked along the East River that day, I prayed, "Lord, if it is ever possible, I would love to live with sunshine streaming into my home. I know this is not a need, just a desire, but Your Word tells me to ask, so I am asking for this, if it is according to Your will."

My prayer for sunshine might seem like a petty desire to some, but the fact that God answered that prayer reminded me once again of how He does not forget or ignore the prayers of His children. He remembers them, and He answers them in His way and in His time to accomplish His purposes. On His way to answering that prayer, He answered so many other prayers—even prayers we hadn't known to utter—and changed my and Billy's hearts in ways we wouldn't have believed if either of us had been told on that sunny day in New York City seven years prior.

But God works in bigger and better ways than we can ask or even imagine. He even gives us the things we don't ask for but that He wants to give to us. Think back to King Solomon. The Lord appeared to him in a dream and said, "Ask for whatever you want me to give you" (1 Kings 3:5 NIV). Solomon could have asked for *anything*, but what did he ask for? "Give your servant therefore an understanding mind to govern your people, that I may discern between good and evil" (v. 9). Solomon wanted wisdom. I love what happened next:

> It pleased the Lord that Solomon had asked this. And God said to him, "Because you have asked this, and have not asked for yourself long life or riches or the life of your enemies, but have asked for yourself understanding to discern what is right, behold, I now do according to your word. Behold, I give you a wise and discerning mind, so that none like you has been

before you and none like you shall arise after you. I give you also what you have not asked, both riches and honor, so that no other king shall compare with you, all your days. And if you will walk in my ways, keeping my statutes and my commandments, as your father David walked, then I will lengthen your days." (1 Kings 3:10–14)

Am I saying that my asking for sunshine was the equivalent of Solomon's asking for wisdom? No. But I am saying that God's ways and plans are so much bigger than ours. When we call out to Him and walk in His ways, we will find that He is faithful to us. We don't know how that will happen or what it will look like, but we can rest assured that God "is able to do immeasurably more than all we ask or imagine, according to the power that is at work within us."

Chapter 13

THE PAINS
OF CHANGE

CHANGE IS RARELY EASY, IS IT? It can turn our world upside down, in good ways and in bad ways. And I've found that my family members don't all deal with change in the same way. I'm sure you could say the same thing about your family. God created us all differently, we have different personalities and past experiences, and we're all at different places in our spiritual walk, all of which affects how we deal with change.

Although we knew God had led us to move to Florida, that doesn't mean the move was easy. It was a major adjustment for all of us lifelong New Yorkers. Sure, Billy and I had each spent a few years away from Manhattan when we were in college, but we were New Yorkers through and through, as were the kids. We all experienced differing degrees of culture shock and dealt with our new situation in various ways.

I was excited about the move, because I knew how God had brought it all about and that it was where He wanted us. I also looked forward to living in a house rather than an apartment, which is all I had ever known. Nevertheless, I cried many times before the move, because I was leaving everything familiar behind and basically starting again in what nearly amounted to a foreign land. But I knew God would bring us through it, because it was so clear He had brought us *to* it.

Once we had moved to Florida, I really never looked back. This may sound surprising, but I didn't miss New York. I missed my family, but I didn't miss the cramped apartment living or the winters. We would go back to visit, and my dad and my sister's family would visit us in Florida, but I had found a new home. I knew God had called us there, and an experience soon after moving confirmed it even more. Just after we arrived in Florida, some new friends were going through a tough time with the husband's job, and nearly everyone in their lives turned their back on this couple. Billy and I spent hours with them, talking through it and praying with them. I truly felt that God had sent us to come alongside this couple because they needed someone to walk with them through that difficult time.

That first year was great for our own marriage. It was all new; we were meeting lots of people. We sold the restaurant in New York, so Billy was also embarking on new adventures. During the first year in Florida, he was mainly focused on getting our new house built, and soon thereafter he started his own sports management agency, through which he represents professional baseball players. He did miss New York, though, and every once in a while he would fly up there. "I just need to go to New York," he'd say, and off he would go.

After arriving in Florida, I immediately became involved in the local Bible Study Fellowship class, which I had visited on many previous trips to Fort Lauderdale. Because of my experience in BSF leadership, I was asked to be a discussion leader in the class. I instantly had a group of forty female friends who would do anything for me. It was such a blessing to have a network of friends so quickly, and not just any friends but Christian women leaders who were committed to grow in the Lord. This was also an answer to my prayers, as I had been praying for an older, godly married woman to mentor me. When I am somewhere new, I need to get involved and meet people and serve, and I was so thankful that God had given me this opportunity to serve in BSF upon my arrival in Florida and that He had answered my prayers yet again.

During that year, Billy and I also started speaking together about our experiences. About six months after we moved to Florida, Nancy DeMoss hosted a dinner for pastors at her home in Palm Beach. She asked Billy and me to come and share our testimony. As a result, the pastors of those churches started inviting us to speak. It seemed like God had prepared the way for us and was using us in new ways to serve Him and others.

SIBLING TROUBLE

The kids, however, were not happy about the move. In fact, when we showed them the land where we were going to build the house, Douglas wouldn't even get out of the car. I can't say that I blame him. He was being uprooted from everything he had ever known. He and Courtney had to leave their friends, their schools, and their comfort zone. They were moving from a place where the city was literally at their doorstep, so that they could come and go on their own without much effort, to a place where I would have to drive them everywhere.

When we first talked to Courtney about the move, she was against it; the only thing that made her excited was the thought of being able to ride horses. We quickly found her a place to ride, which greatly helped her adjustment period because she was doing something she loved and hadn't had much opportunity to do in New York.

Douglas had a more difficult time than Courtney did, most likely due to his age. He was older and more established in his friendships and sports teams. In New York he had played varsity soccer, baseball, and ice hockey. When we arrived in Florida, just in time for school to start that August, the only two fall sports available were cross-country and football. He had participated in neither before, and without a sport to play, he was lost. He went from being big man on campus to knowing no one and having no sport. It was extremely tough on him. Thankfully, after school started and the youth group at church began meeting, things picked up for Douglas. He met some friends at church and began to build relationships.

However, Douglas was frustrated by the many changes and the lack of freedom he had in Florida compared to what he'd had in New York. He couldn't just walk, rollerblade, or take the subway to a friend's house whenever the whim took him. He couldn't go anywhere whenever he felt like it. He felt trapped, and unfortunately he began to take it out on his sister.

During our first year in Florida, while our house was being built, we lived in a rental house with rental furniture. Although we had much more space than we'd had in New York, and the kids had their own bedrooms, they had to share a bathroom in the rental house. We finally had to tell Douglas to use the guest bathroom at the back of the house because the kids just couldn't get along. The shared bathroom wasn't the only issue; it seemed that every detail in their lives provoked an argument. Billy and I didn't really know how to help them, and no matter what we tried, we were unable to bring peace between our children. Our efforts at discipline did not bring about changed behavior. We grounded Douglas, took his allowance away, and made him write letters of apology. But nothing we said or did made any difference. The discord between them festered for years.

My heart felt like it had been torn in two. As a mom, I had a great desire for a peace-filled, joyful home. I just wanted my kids to be friends, get along, and be kind and respectful to each other and to us. I was weary and exhausted from constantly being on edge, wondering who would next break the peace and how I could fix it. Billy and I were at odds with each other, too, in trying to find a solution. It occurred to us that Satan, the enemy of our souls, was attacking our children now that Billy and I were reconciled. We finally sought counseling, and I began to fast.

The counselor literally separated the two teens. They were no longer allowed to eat meals together at the same table or in the same room, either at home or in a restaurant. Every other night, one child ate alone in another room. They could not ride in the same car, which meant that either Billy or I had to drive Courtney to school. Douglas drove by himself, as he had his own car by that point, and we could not go in the car anywhere as a family. They could not go to the same activities—even youth group at church. It was a terrible time for us all.

I came to God on my knees, fasting breakfast five days a week, begging the Lord to intervene and to bring healing. I cried and wept before Him because my family was torn apart, and I asked Him for what was humanly impossible. I came boldly, knowing that with God all things are possible (Matt. 19:26), knowing that He rewards those who earnestly seek Him (Heb. 11:6), knowing that He will never stop doing good to us (Jer. 32:40), and knowing that when I trust in Him, He will make my path straight (Prov. 3:5–6). The more I fasted and prayed, the more I was able to relinquish control of the situation and place all my hope in the One who hears and answers prayer, because the more time I spent with the Lord, the more I could truly feel His hand upon me.

This process began during the fall of Douglas's senior year in high school. Just after Christmas, four long months later, a change began to occur. Douglas had undergone nasal surgery the week before Christmas. He was in pain and then acutely uncomfortable for several days. Courtney took pity on him and offered to get him some videos. This seemingly small gesture was huge. Her anger toward and mistrust of Douglas were enormous. She really wanted to have nothing to do with him. She would have been glad if he had disappeared from the face of the earth. Yet she loved her brother and longed for a friendship. She cried out to Billy one night: "I just want a brother to love who loves me and is my friend."

That was the beginning of the change between our children, and it slowly grew. When Douglas left for college in North Carolina the following August, there was still need of healing, but there was an opening in each child's heart. God had moved and responded.

I am grateful to report that, as young adults, our children were able to begin to work through their issues. It has taken time, but the Lord has brought them through it. People who meet them now would never imagine the tumult that once reigned in their relationship. Today they, and their families, live in the same city in North Carolina. They celebrate their birthdays together and babysit for each other, and we often go on vacations together as a whole family. In fact, as I write this, we just returned from an eight-day vacation in a rented beach house in Georgia with the entire family—all eight of us in one house. We cooked and barbecued together, shared the grocery shopping, went bike riding, swam in the ocean, played golf and tennis, worked out at the gym, and, most fun of all, played with our two beautiful grandchildren. Both Douglas and Courtney said it was the best vacation ever. Seventeen years prior, in Hilton Head, when I had cried out to the God I had not yet met, this had been my desire.

All that was truly a work of the Holy Spirit, a direct answer to this mom's times of fasting and years of prayer. Remember Malachi 2:14–15? God speaks about being one with your marriage partner, of *not* breaking faith with the wife of your youth, because God is seeking godly offspring. As Billy and I have worked to stay married, God has given us godly offspring and the family I had always dreamed about.

Hebrews 11:6 says, "And without faith it is impossible to please him, for whoever would draw near to God must believe that he exists and that he rewards those who seek him." God, always true to His Word, has rewarded my family in the most wonderful way, which, in turn, has blessed our marriage!

Chapter 14

A YEAR
OF JUBILEE

IN AUGUST OF 2003, BILLY AND I delivered our second and last child to Wake Forest University for her freshman year. My job description of the past twenty years had come to an end. We were now empty nesters. No more taking kids to school, cooking breakfast on a daily basis, or waving goodbye from the garage. No more, "Mom, what's for dinner?" No more Saturday horse shows. No more power walks with my daughter for exercise. I could only think of the "no mores."

Douglas had left for Davidson College two years before. Billy and I were devastated then, too. We had so much fear of the unknown and so much sadness that an era in our lives had come to an end. Our first-born would be ten hours away by car and beginning the next stage of his life. This is what we had prepared him for and had prayed for, but the reality was incredibly painful. As we said goodbye in the parking lot at Davidson College, Billy had said to Douglas: "I don't care about your grades; I only care that you walk closely with the Lord." And when we returned home, I saw Billy go into Douglas's room morning after morning to get on his knees and pray for him.

Through that experience, God had shown us what He could do and what He had done in Douglas's life. God planted Douglas in a particular dorm on a particular floor with a particular floor advisor, who invited Douglas to Bible study and began to disciple him. Through this relationship, Douglas became serious about his faith and his walk with Jesus Christ. God had shown us mightily that He loved our child and had definite plans for his life. We were grateful and awed beyond words at God's answer to our prayers and realized that this same God loved Courtney as much and had a plan for her life as well.

We left Courtney happy and excited. But as we drove home from the airport and were approaching our house, deep sobs came forth from my innermost being. What would I do with myself with no more kids to attend to? It felt so incredibly empty and bleak. All I could picture were the empty rooms and an empty house—and an empty calendar. I could not imagine any future without my children. I could not see past the hurt and the emptiness.

AN EMPTY CALENDAR

There was nothing on my calendar, because the Lord had impressed upon me the idea of taking a year of Jubilee when I turned fifty that January. In Leviticus 25:10–11 we read how God worked into His covenant law a special year: "Consecrate the fiftieth year, and proclaim liberty throughout the land to all its inhabitants. It shall be a jubilee for you, when each of you shall return to his property and each of you shall return to his clan. That fiftieth year shall be a jubilee for you; in it you shall neither sow nor reap what grows of itself nor gather the grapes from the undressed vines."

The word "consecrate" in the original Hebrew language is *qadas*. It means "to treat as holy" and to be devoted to God, to be withheld from ordinary use and treated as special.[12] So, although the laws and ceremonies of the Old Testament have been fulfilled in Christ, I decided to apply this old covenant teaching and to have my own year of Jubilee. For me, that meant taking a year off from my many ministry responsibilities.

Around the same time of my fiftieth birthday, Courtney also asked me to curtail my ministry commitments, travel, and teaching so that we could spend more time together during her last semester at home. I took this as a confirmation from the Lord to take this Jubilee and to enjoy my daughter's final days before college. It was a "returning to my family property," and it was a ceasing of the "sowing and reaping" of ministry. And so I did. I withdrew from my church's women's ministry, where I had facilitated Bible studies and had been the prayer coordinator for the prior three years.

Withdrawing from the women's ministry was a difficult act of faith. I am a planner and love to know where I am going and what I am doing. I am uncomfortable leaving anything to chance or to the last minute. This step into a year of Jubilee was way outside my comfort zone, but I thoroughly enjoyed my Jubilee time with Courtney. It was such a gift to be able to further build closeness and trust in my relationship with my teenage daughter. I am so grateful to God for giving me the opportunity and encouragement to bond with Courtney on a deeper level.

So heading home from the airport at the end of August, I was returning to an empty house and an empty calendar. My journal entry the next morning read:

Friday, August 27, 2003

Home last night. I cried and cried. I'm very sad, and it feels so different to be in this empty house. Yesterday, all day was fine, fun, and Court was in a great mood. I wasn't even sad until it was time to say goodbye. Then the floodgates opened, and I felt like there was a huge hole in my heart. Billy was so sweet to me. Dougie too. He called two times yesterday to see how we were doing. What a praise!

It truly feels like a death—this big empty place. Help me to grieve in a healthy way, with perspective. We are all so incredibly blessed by You, my gracious Heavenly Father. Praise You!

The next couple of months were painful, and I felt somewhat as though I were in a free fall. However, the one thing I knew for sure each day was that I would spend the first part of my morning in quiet time with the Lord. Now with the kids gone and the calendar empty, I realized I could spend as much time as I needed or wanted in worshiping the Lord through reading my Bible and prayer. Four days after leaving Courtney at college, I wrote in my journal:

> Today is like the first day of a new life. Both kids are away. I didn't need to be at breakfast at 7:15. Please lead me in the use of my time. I must admit, it's kind of fun with just Billy and me. My time yesterday at church was so encouraging. There was so much joy with good friends.
>
> [From Your Word this morning] Psalm 100:1–2: "Make a joyful noise to the LORD, all the earth! Serve the LORD with gladness! Come into his presence with singing!"
>
> As deeply as I grieved Thursday and Friday, today, Lord, I can shout with joy to You! I worship You with gladness. I come before You, singing with joy!

As a matter of fact, spending time with God was the only thing on my calendar. God's Word was ministering to me in a new and deeper way than ever before. I kept asking God, "What am I to do? What do You want me to do? Please show me through Your Word." And finally I heard God whisper: "Sit at My feet." In other words, "Keep doing what you are doing—spending lots and lots of time with Me in My Word." Remembering how Jesus commended Martha's sister, Mary, for sitting at Jesus' feet listening to what He said (Luke 10:38–42) while chastising Martha for being worried and upset about many things (too busy), I was further encouraged to be still. And I was ecstatic and excited and comforted at this God-given direction. Yet a part of me struggled when people asked, "What are you doing now that the kids are gone?"

I just didn't know how to explain what I was doing. That was probably because I didn't yet realize what the Lord was doing in me.

A CHANGE IN MINISTRY

Toward the end of that October, I got an email from Pro Athletes Outreach. They asked if I would be willing to give the devotion talk and prayer at the upcoming board meeting (Billy and I served on the board by that time) before the November Couples Baseball Conference in San Antonio. I was so excited. I had done it the year before, and I thought they had asked me again because I had done a good job. I felt as though it was a confirmation of my teaching gift and a direct encouragement from the Lord. I was definitely in need of encouragement. But God had other plans. Billy had a conflict, and we could not go to San Antonio.

I was devastated. Finally there was something tangible to do, and I was not going to be able to do it. I knew God was sovereign over this situation, but I was still shattered. And then immediately God showed me my deep pride and desire for recognition. He led me to repentance of needing outward recognition and approval. I was so deeply saddened that I wanted to teach about God in order to receive personal acclaim.

October 27, 2003

I seem to find my significance in what I'm doing instead of in You. Please change that in me. All I am is because of who You are and what You have done. God, please forgive me for having it backward.

October 28, 2003

As for me, please help me to rest in You and to accept this assignment [of quietly sitting at Your feet without any agenda]. I feel so much like I should be doing something—go to school, get a graduate degree, teach a Bible study, write. Oh, please direct me to what You want and to enjoy this time and flexibility. "Those who honor me I will honor." Oh, Lord Jesus, I am so sorry that I have such a hard time being still.

Right then and there I said to the Lord, "I will do nothing but sit at Your feet if that is what You want. I do not want to do anything for my own gratification, for my own need, or for my own acclaim. I will not do anything now, Lord, until You bring it to me. I will not seek a job or a project unless You show me that it is from You and for You— period! I surrender all my time to You." I felt an immediate relief, release, and joyful freedom. I was no longer in charge. I belonged to God, my time belonged to Him, and if He wanted me to do anything, He would open the doors He wanted me to walk through and shut those He didn't. Until then, I would follow Psalm 46:10: "Be still, and know that I am God."

A few weeks later, a young woman came up to me in church and asked me to be her mentor. I knew immediately that I was to do it. This young woman had been divorced from her husband, and then they had both come to know Jesus and had remarried each other. Their circumstances were so similar to ours, and God was directly encouraging me by allowing me to mentor and encourage my friend.

Around the same time, my pastor preached a sermon series on leadership. He explained that leaders make a difference through their faith, in their family and for the future. They don't let dreams die, even when trials come. And God equips those He calls to do the work He has called them to do. Through this, God birthed in me a deep desire to come alongside women struggling in their marriage, to encourage them and to point them to God.

Then another difficult marriage was brought to my attention. Before I knew it, I was working with three women in the midst of difficult marriage situations. God had given me a ministry. *He* had brought these women to me. I had pursued nothing. It was so clear to me that God was leading and that, finally, I was following. It was a joyful realization that God truly had a plan for me—a plan to speak into the lives of women who struggle in their marriage—and that He had not forgotten me. It was a true time of joy after a true time of refining. I knew I had been through the refiner's fire, as God sloughed away more of my old baggage and self-reliance. And how powerfully He had shown me how He delights to do good to His people, that He loves them with an everlasting love, and that He has a plan for their good and not for evil, to prosper them, and to give them a future and a hope. Through the barrenness of the fall, I had clung to the verses that promise those things, and God had proved them true and brought springtime into my life.

By Christmas, I was sensing a new work and direction. I had made one ministry commitment during my Jubilee year, to serve as the prayer coordinator for my church's women's conference. Actually, I had turned down the job, trying to be faithful to the Jubilee. But as I meditated on Scripture, accepting this one task had seemed right and good. I had held this position previously, but now, with little else on my calendar, I was able to do a more thorough job, praying daily for the conference. I had a new freedom and joy during this time that I had never before experienced in my walk with God. I felt free to be exactly who God created me to be without worrying what anybody thought. I was no longer trying to downplay my personality or even change how I dressed. I just began to know God's love and acceptance in a new and profound way.

Then, on conference day, I ran into a friend who is a writer. I told her that several people had told me I needed to write a book about our story, but I felt that I wasn't a writer and was clueless about how to begin. I asked if she would write it for me, but she encouraged me to write the book myself. "Just start writing your story, and you will see. It will evolve," she counseled. I marked off two days a week to start writing, which I did. Though it has been a long process, you are now reading what began as a seed at the end of my year of Jubilee.

STEPPING DOWN FROM THE THRONE

God had a definite plan for my year of Jubilee. As I look back over the journey the Lord took me on during that year, I am overcome with awe at all He did in my heart, which spilled over into my marriage. God was working to purify and heal me. On the day of Courtney's graduation—thirty-two years and four days after my own—I wrote in my journal:

> I am so excited for Courtney. You, Lord, have reminded me of my own graduation, just six days after Mom died. So different from this. Today is a gift from You that so far exceeds the hurt and pain of June 1971. . . . Thirty-two years later, making me the mom I always wished I'd had and giving me the most precious daughter who loves You. You have blessed me far beyond anything I could have asked or imagined. Thank You, Lord!

Shortly thereafter, I began reading *Brokenness: The Heart God Revives* by Nancy Leigh DeMoss,[13] and God began showing me my sins: self-righteousness, self-centeredness, selfishness, perfectionism, pride, and idolatry, just to name a few. (Note that "self" is prevalent in this list, revealing that there is too much focus on myself and not enough on God.) I started to realize that I had been seeing Billy's sins and demanding that he change, but I had not been looking at my own sins. I was seeing the splinter in his eye but not the plank in my own (Matt. 7:3). This required me to seek God's forgiveness and ask God to help me change. He led me to repentance, as I began to be dissatisfied with my behavior and attitudes.

God also taught me something about idols. Exodus 20:4–5 states, "You shall not make for yourself a carved image, or any likeness of anything that is in heaven above, or that is in the earth beneath, or that is in the water under the earth. You shall not bow down to them or serve them." I had always thought of an idol as a wood or metal image or statue that you could literally bow down to. However, I learned that an idol is anything or anyone we worship instead of God, hoping it will answer our prayers and do our bidding. God showed me that I had been unknowingly elevating Billy to idol status in my heart. I was asking Billy to fill me in the places of my neediness and hurt, but it wasn't working, and it was making me angry. But this is not a husband's job. God alone can fill the emptiness and heal the hurts.

Through this time of refining and discovering that I was attempting to get my needs met outside of God, my contentment began to stem from God Himself. I finally understood that the concept of "my spouse should make me whole" is just a myth. Billy couldn't fill my emptiness, and he is not—nor should I expect him to be—perfect. Once God changed my thinking about this, there was not so much pressure on each of us to be the perfect spouse. What a relief!

I was reminded of Jonah, who went to Nineveh (via the belly of a large fish) to tell the people that God would destroy them if they didn't repent of their wicked ways. When the king heard Jonah's message, Scripture says, "he stepped down from his throne and took off his royal robes" (Jonah 3:6 NLT). That was exactly what I needed to do: step down from the throne of our marriage, stop envisioning Billy on that throne, and leave the throne for God and God alone.

It took a year of Jubilee in order for me to see this concept clearly and to put myself, Billy, and God back in our proper places. If you have the wrong person on the throne, it might not take a year of Jubilee to allow you to see it and make the changes that need to be made, but I want to challenge you to seek the Lord to see if you have put anyone on the throne other than Him. Once you get that straight, your marriage can thrive, just like ours has.

Chapter 15

IN SICKNESS
AND IN HEALTH

BILLY AND I HAVE HAD OUR SHARE of problems over the
years—drugs, affairs, anger, years of separation. If you're reading
this book, you've maybe experienced some of those as well. But maybe
that's not what has put a strain on your marriage; maybe it has been
something neither of you could control, such as health. I know first-
hand that health problems can bring up a whole host of other issues.
We discover who we truly are—and who our spouse truly is—during
times of intense physical pain and emotional stress. Health issues can
break a marriage. But they can also make a marriage—make it stronger,
make it more godly, and make both partners more Christlike. It's not
easy, but it's worth it.

In the spring of 2004, I had to rush Billy to the hospital one morning due to a kidney stone. After he was medicated for the intense pain
and I'd waited for him to get a CT scan and X-ray, I pulled out my one-
year Bible and read the four passages for that day, one each from the
Old Testament, the New Testament, a psalm, and a proverb. God gave
me the following words of encouragement and direction from each
passage. I share them with you in the hope that they will also help you
when your husband or other loved one is hurting.

"Listen closely to what I am saying. That's one consolation you can give me" (Job 21:2 NLT). Job, in the midst of his suffering, was telling his friends that they needed to listen to him, not tell him why he was suffering. This was God's clear word and reminder to me that morning as Billy lay suffering and in great pain, that I should not preach at him or give him reasons for his suffering. Instead I should just listen and try to comfort him simply by being there. I would often rather give advice than listen, and I knew that God was giving me an opportunity to practice listening.

"You can be sure the more we suffer for Christ, the more God will shower us with his comfort through Christ" (2 Cor. 1:5 NLT). I knew that God meant that He would comfort both Billy and me through this trial. And to think that this exact verse was part of that day's reading was incredibly encouraging. And as I read these words, I felt the comfort, love, closeness, and protection of the Lord. I felt it throughout the day and the next day; it was truly supernatural.

"But may all who search for you be filled with joy and gladness in you. May those who love your salvation repeatedly shout, 'The LORD is great!'" (Ps. 40:16 NLT). As I read this verse, my pain ebbed, and I was filled with both joy and gladness. Yes, Billy was the one in physical pain, but my heart ached for the agony he was in.

Psalm 40:17 says this: "As for me, since I am poor and needy, let the Lord keep me in his thoughts. You are my helper and my savior. O my God, do not delay" (NLT). And so God spoke to me for Billy, too; the God of the universe, the Creator of all things, was thinking about my husband right at that moment when Billy was truly poor and needy. What encouragement to know God was involved in this process so personally and that I could rest in Him and trust Him.

Throughout that long, agonizing day, our pastor came to sit and pray with us, and our friends Brian and Connie also stopped by to pray. After they left, the doctor told me Billy would need two surgeries— one immediately to move the stone out of the passageway and another in a few weeks, at a specialized "stone center," to blast the stone, making it smaller and able to pass. Without hesitation, I said that having two surgeries was not a good idea because Billy has high blood pressure and adverse reactions to anesthesia. I asked Dr. Schneider to do both procedures at the same time. He said it would be close to impossible to move Billy to the other hospital and to get a surgery slot there on such short notice. I insisted that he try. He was not pleased, but as he left, he agreed to see if it would be possible.

Immediately I called Connie and gave her the updated prayer request—that God would make an all-in-one procedure possible. Then she called our entire Bible study small group and asked them to pray. I told Connie that I knew God was already acting on Billy's behalf. I am usually compliant when someone in authority offers a plan, so I sensed that my insistence had to have been the Lord.

I then began singing praise songs to myself while listening to my iPod and needlepointing. For the next two hours, as Billy slept, I relaxed and praised God for His sovereignty over this entire situation (Rom. 8:28). I praised Him because He has promised to bring good from this (Rom. 8:28), because He has promised never to leave or forsake Billy or me (Heb. 13:5), because He is near (Ps. 145:18), because He loves us with an everlasting love (Jer. 31:3), and because He chose us before the beginning of time (Eph. 1:4; 2 Tim. 1:9). I prayed and asked Him to make the one surgery possible, to protect Billy through all the medications they were giving him, to heal Billy, and to give me strength, wisdom, grace, compassion, and much more (Col. 3:12). Through this process of praying and praising, God gave me peace and a quiet joy.

Then the doctor's office called to confirm that Billy would have one surgery the next morning. I practically jumped out of my seat and shouted to the Lord. God had answered my prayer. Early the next morning, Brian and Connie sat with me in the waiting room until the doctor came to give his report of a successful surgery. They left a little later, and I started talking to the other woman in the waiting room. I began to share with her Jesus and His great love, but she told me she was basically uninterested in God and did not believe in His existence. Before I was finished, the nurse came and called me to the recovery room. I gave the woman one of Billy's PAO cards (a baseball card with his picture, on which he shares his life story and the truth that life apart from Jesus Christ is without meaning), and I silently prayed for God to open her eyes, soften her heart, and lead her to Himself.

A week later, I got a follow-up call from a nurse named Karen. After asking the standard questions about Billy's recovery, she asked me if she could ask a personal question. Karen told me the other woman from the waiting room had given her the PAO card. Karen had then shared it with her ten-year-old son, who had shared it with his Jewish neighbor. She asked if I could send her more cards. She said, "I, too, am a Christian, and God is using your husband's testimony in my neighbor's life." I said to Karen, "How faithful God is to use what Billy went through for good and to lead someone to Himself." I was overjoyed.

As Billy began to feel better, he thanked me many times for taking such good care of him, for being there every moment, and for getting him through. He truly saw my love for him—my love in action. We both realized from this experience that our marriage was worth every moment of struggle. There's a depth, a trust, and a peace and comfort to having a life's mate and best friend as you face health issues. From this episode, we both emerged even more secure in our relationship. Billy had completely entrusted himself to me to take care of him, and he had seen my love and compassion in action.

TRAINED BY GOD'S DISCIPLINE

In 2008 Billy came down with a nerve disease that affected his mouth. It has been the most painful thing he has ever experienced—even more than the kidney stones. First, his teeth started to hurt, and several had to be pulled. He developed a nerve inflammation that grew worse and worse. To deal with the pain, he started drinking a lot and taking painkillers. For more than a year, he was in terrible pain, and he was hospitalized twice. It wore him out, and it wore me out too, in my effort to support him.

While visiting New York during that time, we attended services at our New York City church one weekend. The pastor preached a sermon on becoming more like Christ in our walk with God. He used Hebrews 12 in his talk, and as I listened, I knew God was speaking directly to me, because God had been reminding me of the truths of Hebrews 12:1 for a long time: "Therefore, since we are surrounded by so great a cloud of witnesses, let us also lay aside every weight, and sin which clings so closely, and let us run with endurance the race that is set before us."

Hebrews 11 outlines the heroes of Scripture who walked closely with God and were commended for their faith. Then, at the beginning of Hebrews 12, we are challenged to live as they did—by faith, with perseverance and endurance. We are to "throw off everything that hinders and the sin that so easily entangles" (v. 1, NIV)—to stop committing sin, especially those persistent sins in our lives, whatever they may be. I knew these verses by heart, and on many sleepless nights I would repeat them to myself. Each time I came to verse 1, I sensed that God was showing me a deep sin that I was disregarding and that was a problem in my life and marriage: I carried a deep disrespect for my husband, which revealed itself in my lack of biblical submission to him (see Eph. 5:22–24, 33). While it may not have been evident to others, I knew deep down that it was a problem.

I finally prayed that God would enable me to live those verses about submission from Ephesians 5. I wanted to be obedient to God, thereby living free in Him. I wanted to be healed of my hurts, to be able to trust God in the storm, and to be able to love, respect, and submit to my husband in the ways God desired. I wanted my life to be a witness for God so that those who don't know Him would be drawn to Him. Luke 6:43–45 (NLT) says, "A good tree can't produce bad fruit, and a bad tree can't produce good fruit. A tree is identified by its fruit. Figs are never gathered from thornbushes, and grapes are not picked from bramble bushes. A good person produces good things from the treasury of a good heart, and an evil person produces evil things from a treasury of an evil heart. What you say flows from what is in your heart."

I didn't like what was in my heart. I wasn't producing good fruit when it came to my marriage. I knew my thoughts, feelings, and attitudes toward my husband were wrong, and I couldn't seem to change them. I felt like a hypocrite, and I hated it. I hated it for Jesus' sake, because He has given me everything, including His own life. I wanted my life to honor and reflect Him to others so that they too might know of His incredible love. I also hated it for Billy's sake. He doesn't deserve a wife who isn't wholly devoted to him, which I knew is what God commanded of me, both as Billy's wife and as God's child.

I thought of 1 Corinthians 13: "Love is patient, love is kind. It does not envy, it does not boast, it is not proud. It does not dishonor others, it is not self-seeking, it is not easily angered, it keeps no record of wrongs. Love does not delight in evil but rejoices with the truth. It always protects, always trusts, always hopes, always perseveres" (vv. 4–7 NIV). Contrarily, I was easily angered, self-seeking, mistrustful of Billy, and full of pride and self-righteousness. God also reminded me of Ephesians 5:33: "Let the wife see that she respects her husband." I was not doing any of that! I taught it on a consistent basis, and I had done it at times, but I wasn't living it out consistently in that situation.

So I pleaded with God to help me do whatever it would take to change my heart. One of the things He did was lead me to Celebrate Recovery (a Christ-centered, twelve-step program) to find healing for my own issues.[14] Through this program, God helped me to see *my part* and the unrealistic expectations of others that I carried and how doing so adversely affected my marriage. Along with this realization, God brought deep healing. My eyes were opened to the fact that Billy, too, had persevered in our marriage and that everything was not his fault.

During that time I also spent five days at an abbey in Iowa, where I fasted and sought the Lord. When I arrived, I had believed our ministry and testimony were completely blown by Billy's choices for dealing with pain and my angry response to it. I felt that our lives were falling apart. But after five days of prayer, meditating on God's Word, and fasting, I came away from my time at the abbey with a new peace about my marriage and with a new understanding of how deeply God loves me. I had never truly understood that so fully, and it was a great gift.

Hebrews chapter 12 continues:

> And have you forgotten the exhortation that addresses you as sons? "My son, do not regard lightly the discipline of the Lord, nor be weary when reproved by him. For the Lord disciplines the one he loves, and chastises every son whom he receives." It is for discipline that you have to endure. God is treating you as sons. For what son is there whom his father does not discipline? If you are left without discipline, in which all have participated, then you are illegitimate children and not sons. Besides this, we have had earthly fathers who disciplined us and we respected them. Shall we not much more be subject to the Father of spirits and live? For they disciplined us for a short time as it seemed best to them, but he disciplines us for our good, that we may share his holiness. For the moment all discipline seems painful rather than pleasant, but later it yields the peaceful fruit of righteousness to those who have been trained by it. Therefore lift your drooping hands and strengthen your weak knees, and make straight paths for your feet, so that what is lame may not be put out of joint but rather be healed. (vv. 5–13)

These verses jumped out at me during our pastor's sermon. It was obvious to me that we were in the process of divine discipline, which is evidence of God's divine love. But the hope presented in these verses astounded me. Verse 10b states, "God disciplines us for our good, that we may share his holiness." This gave me cause for joy, that in the midst of trial God was going to make us more like Him and, in fact, allow us to share in His holiness.

In Matthew 5:48 Jesus commands us to be perfect, as our heavenly Father is perfect. This is a radical call, not to be perfect in the sense that we never sin but to be a disciple, which is to be transformed in the process of becoming more Christlike. We cannot find this holiness, or perfectness, without our broken places first being healed. That's exactly what God was doing in Billy and me. This process brought each of us to a broken place in our lives, allowing past wounds to surface and be out in the open and have the opportunity to be healed.

We were also being trained by God's discipline (v. 11). Wow! God loved us so much that He used our issues, healed us, and allowed us to come even closer to Him, ridding us of persistent sin in the process. That's real, life-change training, and we both emerged changed and hopeful for the future.

Also at this time, I attended the True Woman '10 conference in Chattanooga, Tennessee. Charlotte Patrick, whom I had met at Campus Crusade Staff Training in 1989—that stranger who had prayed for my marriage nineteen years earlier and whom I hadn't seen since— met me there. Once again, she was like an angel sent by God when I was in a desperate time of need. At the conference, a blind woman shared a story that rocked my world. As she was going blind in her late teens, she cried out to God to remove her blindness, and she shared God's response with us. He told her through His Word: "My grace is sufficient for you, for my power is made perfect in weakness" (see 2 Cor. 12:9). Through that testimony God was teaching me that He is the One who will give me treasures in dark situations in my life and that my contentment does not depend upon my circumstances.

Too much of my happiness was still dependent on what was going on in my life, and on whether my children were doing things well or whether Billy was acting in a way that I wanted. This had to change.

God alone can satisfy. He alone can give joy amidst uncertainty. And I now wanted to live that truth, not just know it. Through Billy's illnesses, God was giving me the opportunity to walk this out.

A BRAND-NEW MARRIAGE

That time was really rough for both of us, even after God began changing my heart. I wondered if Billy would relapse again and if I would find myself relapsing into fear and anger. But I had to learn that I had no control over what he did. I had to trust that God would be with me no matter what Billy chose to do or not to do. I had to let Billy trust God for himself, without me micromanaging him, and I had to understand that God loves Billy just as much as He loves me.

During the following months, we spent a lot of time with a Christian counselor, and God brought us through it all with a brand-new marriage. We came out of that experience with an incredible amount of love and trust, and we truly began to see each other as best friends. There had been some gaps in our relationship before that, but God showed us those gaps and helped us fill them with what He knew was best for our marriage. I was able to share my thoughts and feelings with Billy like I never had before, and he began to listen to me in a way he had never done. God revealed my ignorance and pride in my belief that I was more spiritual than Billy and in the fact that I felt I was always right and Billy was always wrong. God brought me to repentance and to a place of godly submission to both Him and my husband. That's not to say that I never fail anymore, because I definitely do. The difference is that I now realize it and hate when I hurt Billy and sin against God, and I have the desire to get rid of my sin, repent of it, and heal my relationships.

Even though I know God could have spared us the pain of Billy's health issues, it is plain to see that He worked mightily through those times. Did we encounter those painful seasons simply because God wanted to use them to teach us something that He couldn't have taught us any other way? Perhaps, but we'll never know. But I do know that Romans 8:28 is true: "And we know that for those who love God all things work together for good, for those who are called according to his purpose." Through all we have experienced, God has worked for my good and Billy's good, for the good of our marriage, and even for the good of our family, because we love Him.

Chapter 16

AN ISSUE OF RESPECT

THE ISSUE OF RESPECTING MY husband is one of the hardest things I've had to learn in my marriage. As I've talked to women around the world, I know that it is not something that just I struggle with—it is a universal battle for women. It is often difficult to have and show respect for a fellow sinner—a sinner we live with and know better than anyone else in the world. But we are commanded to respect our husbands, so we need to understand why it's important and figure out how to change our thoughts and attitudes toward our husband.

When Billy and I first were married, I didn't know what respect was—not just respect for my husband but respect for anyone, including myself. What I've learned since knowing the Lord is that respect means "to consider worthy of high regard, esteem."[15] Respect allows the other person to safely fail. It says, "I trust you." Respect even includes something as small as not rolling your eyes at another's actions or words. Respect is a choice; it is not based on what someone does but on who he or she is—a person created by God.

Ephesians 5:33 says, "However, let each one of you love his wife as himself, and let the wife see that she respects her husband." A husband's number-one need is that his wife respect him, just as a wife's top need is that her husband love her. You might say, "He's not loving me, so I will not respect him." Or maybe you think, "He doesn't deserve my respect." I have said both of these things, and that brought only misery to my marriage.[16]

SUBMISSION IS A MUST

You already read some of my thoughts and beliefs about biblical submission, and you will read more, but I must also include that topic in this chapter on respecting your husband. In fact, Ephesians 5:33 comes at the end of a larger passage about biblical submission. That passage is not limited to the submission God requires between a husband and a wife; it also applies to that between children and parents, slaves and masters, and two believers. Please hear me when I say that submission does not mean inferiority; it is not a punishment for wives, and it is not solely required of wives. In each of the relationships mentioned in Ephesians, God commands one person to submit to another, but He also has requirements for the second person that are just as important.

To wives and husbands Paul states, "Wives, submit to your own husbands, as to the Lord. For the husband is the head of the wife even as Christ is the head of the church, his body, and is himself its Savior . . . Husbands, love your wives, as Christ loved the church and gave himself up for her" (Eph. 5:22–23, 25). Both partners have a role to play in submission. Both are serving the Lord in their unique marriage roles.

When Paul says, "Submit yourselves to your own husbands as you do to the Lord," he's not saying that women are to submit to their husbands in the exact same ways that they submit to God. Instead, when a wife submits to her husband, that is her service or obedience "to the Lord." While both men and women are created equally in God's image (Gen. 1:26–28), the submission required by God is offered in deference to ultimate leadership, which God has assigned to the husband.[17] Likewise, the husband's role is in service. Just as Christ serves the church by protecting her, so a husband serves his wife by protecting her. That is a tall order for husbands and one that deserves a wife's respect, and, frankly, it brings me peace to know that this is the task God has for my husband—and not for me!

Though submission is a major part of respecting your husband, that isn't all that is entailed in the issue of respect. It goes far beyond submitting to his headship over your marriage and family. Hopefully, my experiences will help you see what respect should—and shouldn't—look like in a biblical marriage.

RESPECT IS AN ACT OF THE WILL

A few years ago when Billy was really sick, I found myself caught in a bad cycle, when I condemned him for his every move. We were constantly bickering, and I was hostile toward any suggestion he made. I was looking only at the negative—which was mostly that he was *being* negative all the time—and it made me want to scream. I would say, "Could you just say something positive instead of telling me all day how awful you feel and how terrible things are?" I told him that he was giving himself the wrong messages and that he wouldn't feel so awful if he stopped thinking and complaining about it all the time.

Looking back, I can see that I was trying to be the Holy Spirit in Billy's life. I didn't know how he was really feeling; I didn't know the root of his sickness. I just wanted things to get better—for him and for me. What I didn't consider for a while was that I couldn't control what Billy said and did. I could only control myself. I finally asked God for help. In His grace, He allowed me to be very sick for twenty-four hours. I had my head over the toilet for an entire night, and as I cried out for God to heal me, I was made to realize that Billy felt that way all the time.

I cried out to God for forgiveness for my lack of compassion, for judging my husband, for trying to be God for him, and for my utter lack of respect for the man I had married. Then I went to Billy and asked him to forgive me for those things.

Next I asked God, "How can I respond when Billy tells me how awful he feels?" I was basically asking Him, "How can I respect my husband in this situation?" God spoke to my heart: "You can speak My Word back to him; speak verses of healing from My Word."

That very day I looked up a verse on healing. When Billy told me how awful he felt, I said, "and with his wounds we are healed." (Isa. 53:5). The next day I quoted Jeremiah 17:14: "Heal me, O LORD, and I shall be healed." Within twenty-four hours, the dynamic had changed. Within forty-eight hours, Billy was cheerful instead of depressed. He was loving toward me again, and I was respectful of him.

God commands us to respect our husbands because, while it's easy to love with our emotions, respect is an act of the will. It is a choice. I definitely know how difficult that choice can be. You might think it's impossible, but there's a reason you married your husband. Go back to that reason. What was it that led you to marry him? Even if you can just respect him for one small thing—he's neat and tidy, or he provides well—find one thing to respect and focus on that.

I have seen how my lack of respect for my husband tore him down. And I have seen that now that I have chosen to respect him and *do* respect him, he has been built up. We have such great power over our husbands. They want, need, and love to be encouraged, which is a by-product of respect. Someone has to make the first move in a marriage in which both of you are tearing each other down. It just takes one person to change the dynamic. If your spouse isn't doing it, you can instigate the change.

"THE 30-DAY HUSBAND ENCOURAGEMENT CHALLENGE"

At that same time God was working on me concerning respect for Billy, I realized I would soon have to teach on the topic of respect, and I needed help. I decided to take the "30-Day Husband Encouragement Challenge" that I had heard about on Nancy Leigh DeMoss's *Revive Our Hearts* radio program.[18] The challenge was to say nothing negative about your husband—to him, to yourself, or to others—for thirty whole days. In addition, on each of those days the challenge includes saying one positive thing about him—to him, to yourself, and to someone else. If you can't think of something different every day, you can say the same thing to him every day until you think of something new.

I knew that this was an area God was working on in me, because in addition to this radio challenge, a month earlier my counselor had suggested I memorize and pray Ephesians 4:29 for myself: "Let no corrupting talk come out of your mouths, but only such as is good for building up, as fits the occasion, that it may give grace to those who hear." So God had already been working on me, but I needed more structure to my plan of showing respect to my husband, and the thirty-day challenge was perfect for me, and, perhaps, it will be for you. In our present-day culture, women love to complain about their husbands to anyone who will listen. This bad habit is contrary to everything in Scripture and will serve only to tear apart a marriage.

The challenge helped me to come up with ideas of what to say to and about my husband each day, because, if left on my own, I would have had some trouble, at least in the beginning. I was helped by the first day's challenge, which is to voice your gratitude. The Scripture reference is Proverbs 31:11–12: "The heart of her husband trusts in her, and he will have no lack of gain. She does him good, and not harm, all the days of her life." Take a look at the suggestions for day one:

To help you get started, have you ever thanked your husband for choosing you above all other women? He found you attractive as a person and appreciated you. Though many circumstances in your marriage may have changed, let your husband know that you are glad God brought you together and that you want to be a blessing to him for the rest of your marriage. Let him know that he can trust you to be in his corner.

Action Step: Say it out loud. One of the best opportunities to express your gratitude is first thing in the morning. How do you greet your husband each morning? Is he confident in your love? Give him a wake-up call that he'll never forget—a big "I love you" and an "I'm so glad I'm your wife!"

A Wife's Prayer: Heavenly Father, I want to do good to my husband by encouraging him for the next thirty days. Soften my heart to the ways that he has chosen me. Show me how to voice my gratitude for him, and teach me how to be in his corner. [19]

After seven days I was shocked to see how the challenge was working. I had joy, and my steps were much lighter as I walked in obedience to the Lord. After ten days, I noticed even more. I had new joy about my marriage, and so did Billy. He was feeling much better, he was talking about his health much less, and he was more cheerful overall. He wanted me to read him the Bible at bedtime, which was new. And we were having fun together.

After seventeen days, just before Billy had to leave for a weeklong business trip, he told me, "For the first time in thirty-four years, I feel like you really love me." By that time he had also begun asking for my opinion, willingly listening to my suggestions, and actually agreeing with me. And this might seem like a little thing, but it was huge to me: we went for a drive, and Billy asked me what I wanted to listen to on the radio. That was an absolute first. We had always listened to sports talk-radio until I wanted to cover my ears. I had never had a choice.

The challenge not only changed Billy; it also changed me. I saw my husband as a godly man, the man who led us in prayer every morning, the man who provided magnificently for me, wanting to make my life easy. I saw Billy as the amazing husband and father that he truly is. I also had a new desire to place myself under his leadership. For instance, I had always gotten a weekly manicure. I justified spending the money, because Billy spent more than that on TVs. He would give me grief about it, but I did it anyway. So when the price of my manicure went up significantly, it occurred to me to talk to Billy about it and let him decide if it would be okay for me to continue. After all, the breadwinning is in his hands, and he is responsible before God to lead us. For the first time I was completely willing to give up this luxury if Billy asked me to. This willingness to follow my husband in this small area was a first step to following him in much larger areas and was a miraculous change in my behavior.

I now have a habit of asking Billy, "Is there anything I am doing that makes you feel that I don't respect you? What do I need to change?" This really makes a difference. It makes Billy feel respected *and* loved. He knows that I care enough about our relationship and our relationship with the Lord to make sure that I am doing everything I can to show him respect.

Believe me, I know that some of you are in situations where you simply don't want to do anything your husband's way and in situations much more serious than weekly manicures. But if you don't want to do it for him, do it out of obedience to God. That's not really the kind of respect God is calling us to, but it's a good place to start. Respecting your husband will change you, and eventually it will change your attitude toward your husband, and it may change him as well. Your marriage will be renewed in ways you can't even begin to imagine right now.

COVENANT MARRIAGE AT ITS BEST

The dynamic in our marriage has changed partly due to my choice to follow and respect my husband. Though I haven't always felt that Billy is worthy of my respect, I have learned that is not my choice to make. Respect is a biblical command, and by submitting myself to this command, I find that I now truly respect him even without having to make that choice. I used to inwardly criticize parts of Billy's character, but now I have a loving burden to cry out to God for those same issues. However, even if that weren't the case, I know that God demands that

I respect him anyway. I think about it in the same way that I think about submission: since God commands me to respect my husband, I show disrespect for God when I disrespect Billy. But when I respect my husband, I am also showing respect for my Lord. God is honored before my husband and all onlookers when I respect the man I married.

I now tremendously respect Billy—especially in his personal life and in his business acumen—and he loves me as he loves himself, just as we are commanded in Ephesians 5:33. That does not mean that we like each other all the time; we still have our moments! But we have come to the point where Billy can correct me, and I can trust him in it. I know he is looking after my best interest, and I respect his discernment and opinion. And in return, there are times when I can see something that Billy cannot, and he has come to trust my discernment. This is what I had always desired in marriage, though I didn't know how to achieve it. This is what I dreamed of and longed for when I said, "I do." This is truly covenant marriage at its best—both spouses loving the Lord and loving and respecting each other. This is my hope for you.

Chapter 17

MARRIAGE GOD'S WAY

TODAY WHEN I SPEAK AT CONFERENCES and churches and when mentoring younger women, I give a talk called "Marriage God's Way." I use the story of my marriage to illustrate the principles that I believe are the most important for married couples to follow. In fact, on a plane trip last month a young woman, with her head in her hands, sat next to me. When she lifted her head and wiped away tears, I asked her if she was okay, and she shared her story. As our conversation continued, and she asked me what I do, I told her that I travel and speak about marriage God's way. She said, "Would you tell me what that is? I am desperate to know!"

Since you have already heard much of my story, I won't reiterate it here, but I would like to share these principles that I told that young woman on the plane.

SEEK GOD FIRST

The Bible verse I have chosen to base my life on is this: "But seek first the kingdom of God and his righteousness, and all these things will be added to you" (Matt. 6:33). I believe the most important part of a God-honoring, healthy marriage is to seek God first. Don't be concerned with trying to make your spouse seek God first. You can only control what you do, not what he does.

Only God is all-sufficient and can meet all of our needs, including emotional and spiritual needs. No human being can meet all of someone else's needs. God didn't create us with that capacity. He created us with a need for Him first, and that's why He tells us to "seek first his kingdom and his righteousness."

When Billy and I first married, he expected me to meet all of his needs, and vice versa. Since then, we have been learning that seeking God first is not just putting God as number one on the day's to-do list; it means to filter everything we do through the truth that God holds first place in our lives. That includes how I view and treat my husband. In our thirty-seven years of marriage, God has taught us that we each must seek *Him* first, not each other or ourselves. I challenge you to consider whether you're expecting something from your spouse that only God can provide.

READ GOD'S WORD DAILY

For me, the second most important principle for building a strong, godly marriage is to read God's Word every day. In Deuteronomy 8:3 Moses gives instructions to the Israelites for successful living. He says: "And he humbled you and let you hunger and fed you with manna, which you did not know, nor did your fathers know, that he might make you know that man does not live by bread alone, but man lives by every word that comes from the mouth of the LORD." In John 17:17 Jesus prays, "your [God's] word is truth." Psalm 119:9 further instructs: "How can a young person stay on the path of purity? By living according to your word." And Romans 10:17 says: "So faith comes from hearing, and hearing through the word of Christ."

To be a wife who follows godly principles, I must know God's Word. The best way to know God's Word and have it readily available for personal application is through daily reading. While God's Word does not specifically say, "Read the Word daily," I believe the above verses, along with many others—all of Psalm 119; Isaiah 55:11; Matthew 4:4; Colossians 3:16; 2 Timothy 2:15; Hebrews 4:12; and James 1:22—point to reading God's Word every day.

For the past fourteen years, Billy and I have read through a one-year Bible (choosing a different translation each year). We read it separately in the morning, and then, throughout the day, we find ourselves sharing with each other what God has shown us through His Word. It might be a word of encouragement or a sin that has been brought to light. This practice enables me to know both God and my husband better as I see what Billy gleans from Scripture. It opens my eyes to realize that Billy and I are both so different and can have wildly different views of the verses we read each day. It also reminds me that neither of us is necessarily right or wrong; we're just different from each other.

Use the Bible as your how-to manual for life and for your marriage. There is no better place to go. As you read, it is imperative that you believe that every word is true (2 Tim. 3:16) and that God has the answer to your every need or situation. If you don't come to His Word with this mindset, you will shortchange yourself and God. God can and will direct your path (Prov. 3:5–6), but you must believe Him and His Word in order to experience true, lasting change.

I have found that having a specific place to go to read God's Word gives me the strength and comfort from the Lord that carries me through a difficult day, as I learned during Billy's kidney stone ordeal. And as I read daily, I am preparing for the trials that inevitably come. Whether you and your spouse read the same Bible passage each day or a different one, or even if your spouse chooses not to read the Bible at all, there is no better way to begin your day than with the Word of God. As God said to Joshua just after Moses died: "Keep this Book of the Law always on your lips; meditate on it day and night, so that you may be careful to do everything written in it. Then you will be prosperous and successful" (Josh. 1:8 NIV). Commit to making this your practice if it isn't already.

PRAY

The third principle for marriage God's way is centered on prayer. Prayer is important in general, and it's crucial for marriage, and praying God's Word is the most powerful tool.

Isaiah 55:10–11 (NIV) says:

> As the rain and the snow come down from heaven, and do not return to it without watering the earth and making it bud and flourish, so that it yields seed for the sower and bread for the eater, so is my word that goes out from my mouth: It will not return to me empty, but will accomplish what I desire and achieve the purpose for which I sent it.

Did you catch what God said about what will be accomplished? His Word will accomplish what *He* desires, not necessarily what we desire, and it will "achieve the purpose for which [He] sent it." And living a life in which God's will is accomplished is truly the abundant life Jesus promised (John 10:10). God's Word is meant to strengthen us in our lives and in our marriages. Reading it daily is vitally important, and so is praying God's Word back to Him. Praying for your marriage, according to God's Word, puts the problems in God's hands. It's a form of surrender. And God is able—so much more able than you or I—to bring about change that is lasting and good.

There are many resources available to help you pray God's Word. It's also helpful to make your own resources. As you read through your Bible, highlight verses that jump out at you—verses that you sense that the Holy Spirit is speaking to you—and make a list of these verses. Don't think of it as reinventing the wheel; see it as a way to immerse yourself in God's Word and pray it back to Him.

These are some of the verses that I have written on file cards and pray regularly for my marriage. Please use them and tailor them to your marriage, adding to them from your own list:

- Genesis 2:24: Pray that your husband will leave his parents, cleave to you, and become one with you.
- Leviticus 11:45; 1 Peter 1:16: Pray that both you and your husband will become holy as God is holy.
- Deuteronomy 11:13–15: Pray that you and your husband will faithfully obey the Lord God, that He will bless you, and that you will be satisfied.
- 1 Peter 3:1–7: Pray that God will teach you to submit to your husband in a healthy way and that your husband will be considerate and treat you with respect.
- Ephesians 5:22–33: Pray this passage verse by verse, asking that both you and your husband will learn God's way of marriage.

Here are some other verses by topic to help you get started:

- Anger: James 1:19–20; Proverbs 14:17; Ephesians 4:26
- Courage: Romans 8:38–39; Isaiah 41:10
- Faith: Luke 17:5; Romans 10:17; 1 Thessalonians 5:8
- Godly living: Romans 4:5; 6:13–14, 22; 8:3–4, 30

Also ask the Lord to make you a wife of noble character (Prov. 31:10–31), who submits to her husband as to the Lord (Eph. 5:22), and who respects her husband (Eph. 5:33). Pray for your husband's salvation (if he is not a believer; John 1:12), and pray that he will be a man of integrity (Ps. 1), strength, and so on. Pray for oneness in your marriage (Gen. 2:24). Trust me—you will never get tired of praying God's Word.[20]

Billy leads us in prayer *every morning*, before we begin our day. We praise God for who He is; we ask forgiveness for the sin in our lives; and we pray for our children, our friends, those who are ill, and our friends who do not yet know Jesus as Messiah. We take all these burdens and lay them before the Lord God Almighty. We also use Scripture as our prayer manual. This is one of our most bonding practices. It bonds us to God and to each other. It contributes to the oneness that God commands in Genesis 2:24: "Therefore a man shall leave his father and his mother and hold fast to his wife, and they shall become one flesh." Wives, if your husband is not leading you in prayer each day, first pray about asking him and then, if so led, ask: "Would you be willing to lead us in prayer each morning?" The benefits are numerous.

SUBMIT TO YOUR HUSBAND

The fourth principle, which we have touched on already, is one that many wives dread hearing about and trying to follow, but as it is prescribed in Scripture, and since I have experienced the benefits in my own life, I'm going to share it with you once again: "Wives, submit to your own husbands, as to the Lord" (Eph. 5:22). The Scripture goes on to say, "Husbands, love your wives, as Christ loved the church and gave himself up for her" (v. 25). We must also remember that wives have no control over what their husband does, and the command to wives is not contingent upon whether their husband follows the command God has given to him. Wives are to submit to their husband because it is what God deems best, not because they feel their husband deserves it or has earned it.

We need to remember that submission didn't originate with marriage; it first showed up in the garden of Eden, when God told Adam to submit to His commands. He was to work and take care of the garden, and he was *not* to eat of the Tree of Knowledge of Good and Evil (Gen. 2:17). Adam and Eve did not submit to God's authority in the garden, and women have lived under the curse that God put on Eve ever since: "Your desire shall be for your husband, and he shall rule over you" (Gen. 3:16).

Like Adam and Eve, we all dislike the word *submission* as much as we dislike submitting to anyone or anything. In fact, that is exactly what sin is—rebellion toward God. As sinners, we are all rebellious by nature. Yet God commands us to submit.

God is the head over all, and as that head He prescribes: "For the husband is the head of the wife even as Christ is the head of the church, his body, and is himself its Savior" (Eph. 5:23). From Ephesians 5 we see that marriage is meant to be a living, breathing picture of the relationship of Christ and His church. Jesus isn't a heartless dictator, ruling His church with an iron fist. Instead, He chose, in love, to go to the cross and gain forgiveness for all sin, in submission to *His* Father's will. Wives aren't the only spouse who has to submit. Husbands, too, must submit to God, just as Christ did. It's a two-way street, but that doesn't mean we get a pass if we think our husbands aren't submitting to God the way *we think* they should. We must believe that God knows our situation (see Hagar's story, Gen. 16:1–16), that He is just (Deut. 32:4), and that He will make all things right in the end (Rev. 16:7).

God is the author of marriage, and He gets to determine what marriage looks like. Men and women were created different but equal (see Gal. 3:28), yet God assigned the role of headship to the man (Gen. 2:15, 18; 3:16b; Eph. 5:22). Ladies, we show our reverence for and trust in God when we submit to our husbands.

Let me be clear about three things submission does not mean. First, God does not call us to submit to physical abuse. If you are in that situation, remove yourself immediately and seek outside help from your pastor, a church elder, or someone in authority. Second, it does not mean following our husband if he asks us to go against God's Word (Acts 5:29). And, third, submission does *not* mean passively saying to our husband, "Whatever you want, dear," anytime a decision is made. Rather, we are to respond to our husband respectfully, without sarcasm or bitterness. There should be no rolling of the eyeballs and no disrespectful facial expressions or other body language. (I know this is hard, believe me!) We are to listen attentively as they share their thoughts and plans, without correcting or belittling them. When there is a decision that must be made but agreement between the spouses is not forthcoming, that is when the wife tells her husband that she will abide by his decision.

Wives, submission means understanding your power and using it in a way that builds your husband's leadership. After thirty-seven years of marriage, I can tell you that I have discovered that there is joy and peace in submission. When I have submitted to my husband's leadership, God has poured out so much blessing, and He has been glorified.

FORGIVE

Finally, we must learn to forgive. Colossians 1:13–14 points us to the greatest gift God has given us—forgiveness: "He has delivered us from the domain of darkness and transferred us to the kingdom of his beloved Son, in whom we have redemption, the forgiveness of sins." This is not only God's greatest gift to us but also the greatest gift we can offer to our spouse. And further, as I paraphrase verses 20–23, now that I have been reconciled to God through Jesus' shed blood, Christ presents me to God as holy in God's sight, without blemish and free from accusation. So, as we have been reconciled to God, we can forgive and be reconciled to our spouse. When asked the secret of their forty-year marriage, one couple responded: "Being great forgivers."

Every marriage consists of two sinners, and sinners sin. Those who have accepted Jesus Christ as their Lord and Savior have been forgiven everything. Every sin they ever commit—past, present, and future—has been forgiven, based on Jesus' work on the cross. His shed blood paid the penalty for all sinners who repent and surrender their lives to Him (Rom. 3:23; 5:8; 6:23).

These are Jesus' words:

> "Therefore the kingdom of heaven may be compared to a king who wished to settle accounts with his servants. When he began to settle, one was brought to him who owed him ten thousand talents. And since he could not pay, his master

ordered him to be sold, with his wife and children and all that he had, and payment to be made. So the servant fell on his knees, imploring him, 'Have patience with me, and I will pay you everything.' And out of pity for him, the master of that servant released him and forgave him the debt. But when that same servant went out, he found one of his fellow servants who owed him a hundred denarii, and seizing him, he began to choke him, saying, 'Pay what you owe.' So his fellow servant fell down and pleaded with him, 'Have patience with me, and I will pay you.' He refused and went and put him in prison until he should pay the debt. When his fellow servants saw what had taken place, they were greatly distressed, and they went and reported to their master all that had taken place. When his master summoned him and said to him, 'You wicked servant! I forgave you all that debt because you pleaded with me. And should not you have had mercy on your fellow servant, as I had mercy on you?' And in anger his master delivered him to the jailers, until he should pay all his debt. So also my heavenly Father will do to every one of you, if you do not forgive your brother from your heart."(Matt. 18:23–35)

Here Jesus clearly illustrates what happens when one who has been forgiven doesn't forgive the one who owes him. That man was sent back to jail to be tortured. I can attest to the fact that any unforgiveness I harbor toward Billy (or anyone else, for that matter) causes me to become bitter, which is akin to being tortured by my own thoughts. Ask God to forgive you for your unforgiveness, and then ask Him to help you forgive your spouse and anyone else toward whom you have been unforgiving.

Billy often says as we counsel other couples, "I don't see how it's possible to be married without Christ at the center, because knowing Christ forgives every sin I have ever committed—past, present and future—prevents me from holding on to a grudge against Vicki."

THE REFINER'S FIRE

Following these principles and putting our marriage back together has not been simple for Billy and me, but God didn't promise that it would be easy. Instead, He has used our struggles to refine us. Through the trials, the tears, the separation, and all the rest of it, God was honing us and making us more like Him. If that was what it took to get us to the point where we are as believers today, it was worth it, and I thank God for all of it—*all of it*! Standing together as man and wife at two high school graduations, two college graduations, two God-honoring weddings, and the birth of our first two grandchildren has been priceless and a gift from the Lord. Our offspring, to our great joy, are godly (remember Mal. 2:15?). Our marriage has never been stronger, and Billy and I know that we will not give up on each other. We will stay in our marriage and work through whatever situations we might face in the future. God has brought us this far, and we stand upon His promise that He will never leave us or forsake us (Deut. 31:6; Josh. 1:5; Heb. 13:5).

Chapter 18

THE JOURNEY CONTINUES

I HAVE NOW BEEN A BELIEVER IN Jesus Christ for twenty-six years, and we have been back in our marriage for twenty-three years. It has taken every day of every one of those years for Billy and me to grow into the people God created us to be, and we have not yet arrived. We are still in process with the Lord. A wonderful, Christ-centered marriage does not happen overnight. We each need time to mature in our faith individually. Let me repeat that for myself as much as for you, the reader: we each need time to mature in our faith individually. Therefore, we each need patience and a realistic approach to life. And we need to be willing to do whatever it takes as the Lord leads: counseling, friends coming alongside, surrendering personal desires, moving to a new city, getting a new job, and so much more. It takes a willingness by both partners to keep the marriage alive.

This is a journey and does not happen in an instant, though Billy and I would have both liked that to happen. In fact, at the beginning, it seemed like it was taking forever. One summer, about three years after reconciling, we were in Maine for a one-week vacation. One day while playing golf, Billy hurt his knee. The second day we received a call from his dad's housekeeper. Billy's dad had returned home from his weekend jaunt to Atlantic City, and the housekeeper thought he might have had a small stroke. Billy wanted to go home immediately. I could not imagine leaving our vacation; his dad seemed like he would be fine until we returned home in five days after picking up the kids from camp nearby. My position was not at all loving, faithful, or compassionate toward Billy or his dad due to the hurt of our years of separation, bitterness that Billy worked seven days a week, and the fact that we had little time together. I felt unloved by Billy's choices at home, and now our vacation was being ruined. Oh, how selfish I was, and how deeply I was operating from hurt instead of healing and from bitterness instead of forgiveness. I was trying to have a storybook vacation with my husband and greatly anticipated the reunion when we picked up the kids from camp. I had planned and looked forward to this time and had run it over and over in my mind. I couldn't let go of it.

We did fly home for three days to situate Billy's dad. I realized it was the right and necessary thing to do, and I finally apologized to Billy. I was deeply sorry, and I knew I was wrong. We then flew back to Maine to pick up our car so that we could collect Douglas and Courtney from camp. While on that drive, Billy suggested we might not be right for each other and that our marriage was not going to work. I was driving, and I swerved over to the side of the road. I was furious and challenged him to commit fully to the marriage, no matter what we would face, or to bail out right then and there. I had made that commitment when Billy came home three years earlier, but it was clear to me that he had not. And I knew we could not go forward unless we were both committed completely. That day Billy made that commitment to our marriage, on the roadside in Maine. What I thought had been a ruined vacation turned out to be what God used to make our marriage stronger. We placed a stake in the ground that day, agreeing that no matter what lay ahead and what we would face, we were both in the marriage permanently. We were realizing that marriage is not a feeling—that we don't always feel like being married, and that we don't always feel like we are in love—but from that point on, we would always be committed to each other. That was just one step—though a huge one—of *many* we have had to take over the years to get our marriage to the place God wants it to be.

I tell you that change won't happen immediately, not to discourage you but to *encourage* you during those times when it seems that reconciliation, oneness, understanding, or whatever you're seeking seems like it will never happen. It can happen. It *does* happen. My marriage is a testament to that truth. My desire for a godly husband and father and of telling the world about Jesus together has come about. We are living that reality. God has answered our prayers over and above our wildest dreams. As Billy has said, "Vicki and I are walking-and-talking miracles. If Christ can do what He has done in our marriage, I don't think anybody should give up." I truly believe that when we put our marriage into God's hands and live our lives worthy of our calling as His children, He will respond. It won't be on our terms or time frame; it will be on His terms, according to His timetable, which is so much better than we could ever know or understand. In this way, God is glorified.

THE WINDS OF CHANGE

To give you a vivid picture of what marriage can be—and what God can do to change a marriage—I want to share with you a letter my husband wrote to me on my sixtieth birthday. You've read our story, so you know what we have experienced and God has brought us through. This is where we are now:

My Sweetheart,

You are the most precious gift that God has ever given me. We have been through so much together, and you have persevered like none other. My life with you today is beyond anything I could have wished for. God's grace is so abundantly clear in our lives.

You have blessed me with the two most precious children, and now we are even more blessed with the most beautiful grandchildren. After almost thirty-six years, my love for you continues to grow each day. I love waking up with you and having the privilege of praying every morning together, as we pray a blessing and hedge of protection on our family. I love doing things with you, and I love bringing you joy when we do things outside my comfort zone. I love traveling with you and holding hands as we take off and land. And I look forward to each night with you, curling in next to you as we comfort each other.

And now, my love, as we grow old together, you are more beautiful in my eyes than you could possibly imagine. I find you to be the sexiest, hottest, and the most wonderful girl in the world. After all these years, I am still totally smitten. And this boy, with the coat slung over his shoulder when we first met, desires to date you for as long as our precious Savior allows.

Happy birthday, my love. I thank God for you all day long. Bill Rose adores you!

Knowing where we have come from, this is truly a miracle. And it is *true*. This isn't just a husband trying to tell a wife what he thinks she wants to hear on a big day. Billy spoke from the heart, which is clearly not the way things have always been. As I've shared, honest communication did not come naturally for either of us. We both grew up in families where expressing thoughts and feelings was not encouraged— whether they were positive or negative. In fact, when I was a child, I learned not to share my feelings because they were usually not acceptable to my mother, and I would get into trouble. Billy and I both had to overcome our pasts in this and other areas. Through biblical counseling, God showed us that we had to be courageous and learn to really speak the truth and not be afraid of the other's response when we open up. So when I read what my husband wrote to me on my milestone birthday, I was overcome by all the Lord had done in our lives and in our marriage.

You will also notice that Billy said, "I love bringing you joy when we do things outside my comfort zone." What a wonderful display of servanthood! Billy and I are different in almost every way—our interests and inclinations are completely opposite. But we have both learned that marriage is about serving each other.

When I think, "What is Billy doing for me today?" I'm in trouble. I don't mean that in an unhealthy way—as if his needs are more important than mine. But I believe that when each partner chooses to serve the other, the result can only be good. You know that in the beginning of our relationship, Billy and I did everything he wanted and nothing I wanted. In fact, he will tell you that's one of the reasons he married me—because he thought I would do pretty much whatever he needed and wanted. And although that was typically the case at the beginning of our marriage, I didn't do it out of a servant's heart but out of a fearful spirit. I was afraid he would leave me if I didn't. This is not the picture of a healthy marriage.

Since becoming believers, God has shown us a better way—Jesus' way, "[I] came not to be served but to serve" (Matt. 20:28). This is a key biblical principle for marriage. It means that often we do things for or with each other that we don't particularly love to do, but when we choose to serve each other and do them, we have joy and it brings us closer together. Billy sums up this part of our relationship perfectly: "We serve each other sacrificially, not because we expect it."

Billy and I were recently asked how our love and admiration for each other has changed over the course of our marriage. Our answers to that question speak volumes about where God has brought us individually and as a couple.

My husband explained that he had married me because I was hot (his word, not mine!) and, like I said, because he thought I would do whatever he wanted. That's what he loved about me then, but so much has changed. He said, "Vicki has more grace; she's softer. She's a comfort to me. I look to her for advice and wisdom. She's my best friend now; she wasn't when we got married. I think that's the most important thing." He continued, "Marriage is a lot of work, but it is well worth the effort. It is great to go to sleep with your best friend and wake up with your best friend. Marriage is impossible without Jesus in the center, because when you have disagreements, it is impossible not to forgive the other person, knowing that Christ forgives you every day. Marriage can be one of the most special things out there, but it takes a lot of work and a lot of growth—a lot of willingness to change to get to that point." Amen!

For my part, when we were married, I simply saw a guy who liked me and could provide well for me, and I fell in love with that. I had little concern about the way he conducted himself or treated me. I wasn't out looking for someone whom I thought would make a good father, and I wasn't thinking of the future at all. Frankly, I loved the thought of being married and the happiness I thought it would bring me more than I loved or admired specific attributes of the man I was marrying. And after the wedding, I still didn't find much to love about my husband. Thankfully, that has changed over the past four decades. Today, what I love and admire the most about my husband is that he loves and follows the Lord. He leads us in prayer every morning, he prays for our children and their families, he is a man of integrity, he is honest in business (even to his own detriment at times), and he follows godly principles in every way, including loving me as Christ loves the church, which *He* gave His life for. I love that Billy is now my best friend. I wouldn't trade Billy for any other man on this earth.

Oh, how things have changed. God is truly faithful.

ABOVE ALL, TRUST IN GOD

Looking back on my journey with Billy, I am constantly amazed at what God has done. I am in awe of the ways the Lord changed me, changed Billy, renewed our marriage, and made us one. Asking God to make us one—and trusting that He can—has been a huge part of our marriage. This is an ongoing process, still requiring us to work hard, daily making choices to build, not tear down, our marriage. And we know that He will keep us united as one when we trust in Him.

We also know that we must remember that our marriage is a God-given covenant. This covenant relationship is meant to be a picture of Christ's relationship with His church—His bride. We are to be united, not divided, so that the world can see Christ through us. During hard times, we remind ourselves and each other that we are not the enemy—Satan is. He seeks to devour and divide Christian marriages. He will do whatever he can to destroy the picture of Christ and the church that marriage is to emulate. Part of the reason I have written this book is that I want all who are married—and especially all believers—to understand that Christian marriage is a picture of Christ and the church. Keeping this covenant is hard, but we can do it through prayer and perseverance. We have to stand against Satan and remember to be a teammate with our husband, not his enemy. We mustn't let the true enemy divide us and tear us apart. God is so much stronger, and we *must* trust in Him. Our marriages depend on it.

Our 2013 Christmas card

Tyson and Courtney Jeffus, Bill holding Benzion,
Vicki holding Noa, Kaitlin and Douglas Rose

AFTERWORD

WHEN SPEAKING OF GOD'S BLESSING upon Abraham, I have heard it said that God's purpose in blessing one is to bless many. And so it is with this story about our marriage reconciliation and the writing of this book. God has blessed Billy and me and our children beyond anything we could have asked or imagined, and we believe His purpose for blessing us is so that *you* would see that He is able, and so that *you* would turn to Him and trust Him to do the impossible.

I want to share with you a note from a woman who listened to me tell our story to Nancy Leigh DeMoss on *Revive Our Hearts*:

> The first time I heard Vicki's story on *Revive Our Hearts* was a couple of years ago, after I had just left my husband after thirteen years of marriage. Her story gave me the idea of God restoring our marriage. Slowly, God warmed me to that idea. I sent for the CD set of Vicki's story and played it many times. I hung on to the hope it offered me that *God* could restore my failed (second) marriage. Well, today my husband and I are celebrating being remarried almost one year ago. And God definitely wove us back together. . . . I hope others will dare to believe God and give Him time to work a miracle of restoration of marriage in their lives. . . . God is God, and He can do the impossible.

Did you notice that she said, "*God* could restore my failed marriage"? I couldn't restore it; my story couldn't restore it; *she* couldn't even restore it. Our story might prompt people to consider what He wants for their marriage—I hope and pray that it does—but it is *God* who changes those individuals, couples, and marriages. He is the restorer of lives and marriages.

Second Chronicles 16:9 says, "For the eyes of the LORD run to and fro throughout the whole earth, to give strong support to those whose heart is blameless toward him." Ask God for a heart fully committed to Him and for the strength to stay in your marriage in order to honor God. Then be patient. As my father used to tell me over and over, "Rome wasn't built in a day." Intimate marriages that honor God take time and commitment and do not just happen overnight. Please use our story as a springboard and as an encouragement to believe that God is able and is waiting to heal, restore, and repair your relationship as you make the choice to stay in your marriage. Use it to know that God is in the midst of the most hopeless situations and still performs miracles. Use it, dear friend, and stay married, for His glory.

ACKNOWLEDGMENTS

Behind our story are the many who contributed, through prayer and standing with us, to the reconciliation of our marriage and the writing of this book. My gratitude runs deep!

Billy, your courage in agreeing to have our story in print humbles me. Thank you for encouraging me daily, for reading every single word, for praying over me every morning, and for seeking the Lord first in your life so that our marriage is a place of refuge and joy. Thank you for thirty-seven-plus years!

Greg Thornton and the Moody Team—I am deeply grateful for you, for taking a chance with a new author, and for all your work to bring our story to print. Rene Hanebutt and Pam Pugh—thank you for your guidance, integrity, and commitment to excellence.

Thank you Dana Wilkerson—working with you was a blessing and a joy! I am most grateful for your ability to write a story. You have become a dear friend.

Thank you Lydia Brownback for your wisdom, skill, and expertise in editing.

Deborah Kirby—thank you for displaying Jesus in your life so that I was drawn to Him.

Nancy DeMoss—thank you for your ministry to the lost in New York City and for your continuing prayers for my marriage and family.

Don Hodel and the late Barbara Hodel— you are my heroes in the faith. Thank you for sharing your story and His, and leading me to the Savior.

Nancy Leigh DeMoss—thank you for your all-in devotion to Jesus Christ and to women and for giving your life for all of us who need a godly mentor who walks so closely with the Savior. Your love and support for Billy and me was God-sent.

BJ and Sheila Weber, Ron and Patsy Fraser, Norm and Bobbe Evans, and Barbara and Skip Ryan—thank you for allowing God to use you mightily in the restoration of our marriage. Your friendship to us is invaluable.

Jackie Kendall—friend, mentor, prayer partner for the last fifteen years—where would I be without your wise, loving, truthful, armor-bearing friendship, and godly counsel, always pointing me back to Jesus!

Mike Neises and the Revive Our Hearts team—thank you for your help and encouragement and especially your prayers.

DeeAnn Boyd, Elizabeth DeMoss, Mike Jeffries, Mac McConnell, and Debbie Petersen—thank you for reading through this manuscript in the very early days and for your helpful comments and encouragement.

For all those at the DeMoss House who prayed Billy into the kingdom and my marriage back together, I am eternally grateful. Your prayers have been answered beyond what we asked or imagined!

Laura and Jeff Calenberg—for friendship and prayers and for taking my pictures—what a fun afternoon!

My pastors—Larry Thompson and Keith Boyd—thank you for faithfully preaching and living the Truth!

Dan Houmes—thank you for your wise and biblical counsel.

Andrew Indelicato—for all your computer technology expertise for this nontech generation girl.

My Praying Friends—Nicole, Reen, DeeAnn, Connie, Ann, Ellie, Susan, Diane, Toni, Janelle, Mike, Heidi, Jackie, Nancy, Laura, Barbara, Linda, Mac, Marilyn, Melissa, Addie, Olga, Pura, Debbie, Barb, Vicky, and Sheila. Thank you for always wanting to know "How's the book coming?", and how to pray. I could not have done this without you. Your prayers have been answered, and only God knows the depth of my gratitude for each of you.

To my sister, Heidi, I'm so grateful for all your moral support, love, and encouragement, then and now! And I am so thankful God made us sisters!

To Dad, the first believer in the Gage family—thank you for your courage and commitment to Jesus, for praying for me all those wandering years, and for your words of blessing after reading the first draft two months before you went home to be with the Lord: "You must get this published."

To my children and their spouses, Douglas and Kaitlin, Courtney and Tyson: I love you more than you can imagine and am so proud of each of you and your lives walking closely with our Lord. Courtney and Douglas, thank you for reading the early manuscript and for your willingness for your part to be shared. For all your encouragement, prayers, support, and help with pictures and technology and so much more, I am so grateful. You are all a priceless gift from the Lord to me!

And finally, to my Lord and Savior, Jesus the Messiah, thank You for loving us so much, dying in our place for the forgiveness of all our sins, and for choosing us for this miracle and giving us the abundant life, full of purpose and peace. You are the One True God and all praise and glory and honor for this book and our lives, belongs to You.

Appendix 1

BIBLE VERSES
FOR MARRIAGE

THE **VERSES BELOW ARE NOT JUST** meant to read and think, "Oh, how nice." God placed these verses in His Word for us to put to work and to live by.

OLD TESTAMENT

Therefore a man shall leave his father and his mother and hold fast to his wife, and they shall become one flesh. (Gen. 2:24)

You shall therefore be holy, for I am holy. (Lev. 11:45; see also 1 Pet. 1:16)

And if you will indeed obey my commandments that I command you today, to love the LORD your God, and to serve him with all your heart and with all your soul, he will give the rain for your land in its season, the early rain and the later rain, that you may gather in your grain and your wine and your oil. And he will give grass in your fields for your livestock, and you shall eat and be full. (Deut. 11:13–15)

The LORD is my shepherd; I shall not want. (Ps. 23:1)

When words are many, transgression is not lacking, but whoever restrains his lips is prudent. (Prov. 10:19)

A soft answer turns away wrath, but a harsh word stirs up anger. (Prov. 15:1)

And this second thing you do. You cover the LORD's altar with tears, with weeping and groaning because he no longer regards the offering or accepts it with favor from your hand. But you say, "Why does he not?" Because the LORD was witness between you and the wife of your youth, to whom you have been faithless, though she is your companion and your wife by covenant. Did he not make them one, with a portion of the Spirit in their union? And what was the one God seeking? Godly offspring. So guard yourselves in your spirit, and let none of you be faithless to the wife of your youth. (Mal. 2:13–15)

NEW TESTAMENT

It was also said, 'Whoever divorces his wife, let him give her a certificate of divorce.' But I say to you that everyone who divorces his wife, except on the ground of sexual immorality, makes her commit adultery, and whoever marries a divorced woman commits adultery. (Matt. 5:31–32)

Then Peter came up and said to him, "Lord, how often will my brother sin against me, and I forgive him? As many as seven times?" Jesus said to him, "I do not say to you seven times, but seventy-seven times." (Matt. 18:21–22)

And Pharisees came up to him and tested him by asking, "Is it lawful to divorce one's wife for any cause?" He answered, "Have you not read that he who created them from the beginning made them male and female, and said, 'Therefore a man shall leave his father and his mother and hold fast to his wife, and the two shall become one flesh'? So they are no longer two but one flesh. What therefore God has joined together, let not man separate." (Matt. 19:3–6)

And he left there and went to the region of Judea and beyond the Jordan, and crowds gathered to him again. And again, as was his custom, he taught them. And Pharisees came up and in order to test him asked, "Is it lawful for a man to divorce his wife?" He answered them, "What did Moses command you?" They said, "Moses allowed a man to write a certificate of divorce and to send her away." And Jesus said to them, "Because of your hardness of heart he wrote you this commandment. But from the beginning of creation, 'God made them male and female.' Therefore a man shall leave his father and mother and hold fast to his wife, and the two shall become one flesh.' So they are no longer two but one flesh. What therefore God has joined together, let not man separate." And in the house the disciples asked him again about this matter. And he said to them, "Whoever divorces his wife and marries another commits adultery against her, and if she divorces her husband and marries another, she commits adultery." (Mark 10:1–12)

Now concerning the matters about which you wrote: "It is good for a man not to have sexual relations with a woman." But because of the temptation to sexual immorality, each man should have his own wife and each woman her own husband. The husband should give to his wife her conjugal rights, and likewise the wife to her husband. For the wife does not have

authority over her own body, but the husband does. Likewise
the husband does not have authority over his own body, but
the wife does. Do not deprive one another, except perhaps by
agreement for a limited time, that you may devote yourselves
to prayer; but then come together again, so that Satan may not
tempt you because of your lack of self-control. (1 Cor. 7:1–5)

To the married I give this charge (not I, but the Lord): the
wife should not separate from her husband (but if she does,
she should remain unmarried or else be reconciled to her husband), and the husband should not divorce his wife. To the
rest I say (I, not the Lord) that if any brother has a wife who
is an unbeliever, and she consents to live with him, he should
not divorce her. If any woman has a husband who is an unbeliever, and he consents to live with her, she should not divorce
him. For the unbelieving husband is made holy because of his
wife, and the unbelieving wife is made holy because of her
husband. Otherwise your children would be unclean, but as it
is, they are holy. But if the unbelieving partner separates, let it
be so. In such cases the brother or sister is not enslaved. God
has called you to peace. For how do you know, wife, whether
you will save your husband? Or how do you know, husband,
whether you will save your wife? Only let each person lead
the life that the Lord has assigned to him, and to which God
has called him. This is my rule in all the churches. (1 Cor.
7:10–17)

Love is patient and kind; love does not envy or boast; it is not
arrogant or rude. It does not insist on its own way; it is not ir-
ritable or resentful; it does not rejoice at wrongdoing, but rejoices with the truth. Love bears all things, believes all things,
hopes all things, endures all things. (1 Cor. 13:4–7)

Do not be unequally yoked with unbelievers. For what partnership has righteousness with lawlessness? Or what fellowship has light with darkness? (2 Cor. 6:14)

I have been crucified with Christ. It is no longer I who live, but Christ who lives in me. (Gal. 2:20)

And do not get drunk with wine, for that is debauchery, but be filled with the Spirit, addressing one another in psalms and hymns and spiritual songs, singing and making melody to the Lord with your heart, giving thanks always and for everything to God the Father in the name of our Lord Jesus Christ, submitting to one another out of reverence for Christ. Wives, submit to your own husbands, as to the Lord. For the husband is the head of the wife even as Christ is the head of the church, his body, and is himself its Savior. Now as the church submits to Christ, so also wives should submit in everything to their husbands. Husbands, love your wives, as Christ loved the church and gave himself up for her, that he might sanctify her, having cleansed her by the washing of water with the word, so that he might present the church to himself in splendor, without spot or wrinkle or any such thing, that she might be holy and without blemish. In the same way husbands should love their wives as their own bodies. He who loves his wife loves himself. For no one ever hated his own flesh, but nourishes and cherishes it, just as Christ does the church, because we are members of his body. "Therefore a man shall leave his father and mother and hold fast to his wife, and the two shall become one flesh." This mystery is profound, and I am saying that it refers to Christ and the church. However, let each one of you love his wife as himself, and let the wife see that she respects her husband. (Eph. 5:18–33)

Not that I am speaking of being in need, for I have learned in whatever situation I am to be content. I know how to be brought low, and I know how to abound. In any and every circumstance, I have learned the secret of facing plenty and hunger, abundance and need. I can do all things through him who strengthens me. (Phil. 4:11–13)

Put on then, as God's chosen ones, holy and beloved, compassionate hearts, kindness, humility, meekness, and patience, bearing with one another and, if one has a complaint against another, forgiving each other; as the Lord has forgiven you, so you also must forgive. And above all these put on love, which binds everything together in perfect harmony. (Col. 3:12–14)

May the Lord make you increase and abound in love for one another and for all, as we do for you, so that he may establish your hearts blameless in holiness before our God and Father, at the coming of our Lord Jesus with all his saints. (1 Thess. 3:12–13)

Pray without ceasing. (1 Thess. 5:17)

Likewise, wives, be subject to your own husbands, so that even if some do not obey the word, they may be won without a word by the conduct of their wives, when they see yourrespectful and pure conduct. Do not let your adorning be external—the braiding of hair and the putting on of gold jewelry, or the clothing you wear—but let your adorning be the hidden person of the heart with the imperishable beauty of a gentle and quiet spirit, which in God's sight is very precious. For this is how the holy women who hoped in God used to adorn themselves, by submitting to their own husbands, as Sarah obeyed Abraham, calling him lord. And you are her children, if you do good and do not fear anything that is frightening. Likewise, husbands, live with your wives in an understanding way, showing honor to the woman as the weaker vessel, since they are heirs with you of the grace of life, so that your prayers may not be hindered. (1 Pet. 3:1–7)

And this is the confidence that we have toward him, that if we ask anything according to his will he hears us. And if we know that he hears us in whatever we ask, we know that we have the requests that we have asked of him. (1 John 5:14–15)

Appendix 2

SUGGESTED READING LIST AND RESOURCES FOR MARRIAGE

BOOKS

Chapman, Gary. *Covenant Marriage: Building Communication and Intimacy.* Nashville: Broadman, 2003.

———. *The Five Love Languages: The Secret to Love That Lasts.* Chicago: Northfield, 2010.

Cloud, Henry, and John Townsend. *Boundaries in Marriage.* Grand Rapids: Zondervan, 2009.

DeMoss, Nancy Leigh. *Biblical Portrait of Womanhood: Discovering and Living Out God's Plan for Our Lives.* Buchanan, MI: Life Action Ministries, 1999.

———. *Brokenness: The Heart God Revives.* Chicago: Moody, 2005.

———. *Choosing Forgiveness: Your Journey to Freedom.* Chicago: Moody, 2005.

Dillow, Linda, and Lorraine Pintus. *Intimate Issues: Twenty-One Questions Christian Women Ask about Sex.* Colorado Springs: WaterBrook, 2009.

Eggerichs, Emerson. *Cracking the Communication Code: Love for Her, Respect for Him; The Secret to Speaking Your Mate's Language.* Nashville: Thomas Nelson, 2006.

————. *Love and Respect: The Love She Most Desires; The Respect He Desperately Needs.* Nashville: Thomas Nelson, 2004.

Groom, Nancy. *Married without Masks: A New Look at Submission and Authority.* Grand Rapids: Baker, 1996.

Harley, Willard F., Jr. *His Needs, Her Needs: Building an Affair-Proof Marriage.* Grand Rapids: Revell, 2011.

Keller, Timothy. *Counterfeit Gods: The Empty Promises of Money, Sex, and Power, and the Only Hope That Matters.* New York: Dutton, 2009.

————. *The Meaning of Marriage: Facing the Complexities of Commitment with the Wisdom of God.* With Kathy Keller. New York: Riverhead, 2011.

Moore, Beth. *Praying God's Word: Breaking Free from Spiritual Strongholds.* Nashville: Broadman, 2009.

Omartian, Stormie. *The Power of a Praying Wife.* Eugene, OR: Harvest, 2014.

Penner, Joyce J., and Clifford L. Penner. *Men and Sex: Discovering Greater Love, Passion, and Intimacy with Your Wife.* Nashville: Thomas Nelson, 1997.

Piper, John. *This Momentary Marriage: A Parable of Permanence.* Wheaton: Crossway, 2009.

Roberts, Lee. *Praying God's Will for My Husband.* Nashville: Thomas Nelson, 2002.

Rosberg, Barbara, and Gary Rosberg. *The Five Love Needs of Men and Women.* Carol Stream, IL: Tyndale, 2001.

————. *Healing the Hurt in Your Marriage.* Colorado Springs: Focus on the Family, 2004.

Tada, Ken, and Joni Eareckson Tada. *Joni and Ken: An Untold Love Story.* With Larry Libby. Grand Rapids: Zondervan, 2013.

Thomas, Gary L. *Sacred Marriage: What If God Designed Marriage to Make Us Holy More than to Make Us Happy?* Grand Rapids: Zondervan, 2002.

Towns, Elmer, and Jerry Falwell. *Fasting Can Change Your Life.* New

York: Regal, 1998.

Vernick, Leslie. *How to Act Right When Your Spouse Acts Wrong.* Colorado Springs: WaterBrook, 2001.

Wagner, Kimberly. *Fierce Women: The Power of a Soft Warrior.* Chicago: Moody, 2012.

BIBLES

The Daily Walk Bible NLT. Edited by Chip Ingram. Carol Stream, IL: Tyndale, 2013.

The One-Year Study Bible NLT. Carol Stream, IL: Tyndale, 2011.

RADIO

Revive Our Hearts daily radio broadcast. http://www.reviveourhearts.com.

Appendix 3

CELEBRATE RECOVERY'S TWELVE STEPS AND THEIR BIBLICAL COMPARISONS [21]

1. **We admitted we were powerless over our addictions and compulsive behaviors, that our lives had become unmanageable.**

    For I know that nothing good dwells in me, that is, in my flesh. For I have the desire to do what is right, but not the ability to carry it out. (Rom. 7:18)

2. **We came to believe that a power greater than ourselves could restore us to sanity.**

    For it is God who works in you, both to will and to work for his good pleasure. (Phil. 2:13)

3. **We made a decision to turn our will and our lives over to the care of God.**

    I appeal to you therefore, brothers, by the mercies of God, to present your bodies as a living sacrifice, holy and acceptable to God, which is your spiritual worship. (Rom. 12:1)

4. **We made a searching and fearless moral inventory of ourselves.**

   Let us test and examine our ways, and return to the LORD! (Lam. 3:40)

5. **We admitted to God, to ourselves, and to another human being, the exact nature of our wrongs.**

   Therefore, confess your sins to one another and pray for one another, that you may be healed. (James 5:16)

6. **We were entirely ready to have God remove all these defects of character.**

   Humble yourselves before the Lord, and he will exalt you. (James 4:10)

7. **We humbly asked Him to remove all our shortcomings.**

   If we confess our sins, he is faithful and just to forgive us our sins and to cleanse us from all unrighteousness. (1 John 1:9)

8. **We made a list of all persons we had harmed and became willing to make amends to them all.**

   And as you wish that others would do to you, do so to them. (Luke 6:31)

9. **We made direct amends to such people whenever possible, except when to do so would injure them or others.**

   So if you are offering your gift at the altar and there remember that your brother has something against you, leave your gift there before the altar and go. First be reconciled to your brother, and then come and offer your gift. (Matt. 5:23–24)

10. **We continued to take personal inventory and when we were wrong, promptly admitted it.**

    Therefore let anyone who thinks that he stands take heed lest he fall. (1 Cor. 10:12)

11. **We sought through prayer and meditation to improve our conscious contact with God, praying only for knowledge of His will for us, and power to carry that out.**

    Let the word of Christ dwell in you richly. (Col. 3:16)

12. **Having had a spiritual experience as the result of these steps, we tried to carry this message to others and practice these principles in all our affairs.**

    Brothers, if anyone is caught in any transgression, you who are spiritual should restore him in a spirit of gentleness. Keep watch on yourself, lest you too be tempted. (Gal. 6:1)

Appendix 4

THE WAY TO SALVATION

1. **Everyone needs salvation because we have all sinned.**

   As it is written: "None is righteous, no, not one; no one understands; no one seeks for God. All have turned aside; together they have become worthless; no one does good, not even one." . . . for all have sinned and fall short of the glory of God. (Rom. 3:10–12, 23)

   Indeed, there is no one on earth who is righteous, no one who does what is right and never sins. (Eccl.7:20)

2. **The price (or consequence) of sin is death.**

   For the wages of sin is death, but the free gift of God is eternal life in Christ Jesus our Lord. (Rom. 6:23)

   The one who sins is the one who will die. (Ezek. 18:20)

3. **Jesus Christ died for our sins. He paid the price for our death.**

   But God shows his love for us in that while we were still sinners, Christ died for us. (Rom. 5:8)

   But he was pierced for our transgressions, he was crushed for our iniquities; the punishment that brought us peace was on him, and by his wounds we are healed. (Isa. 53:5)

4. **We receive salvation and eternal life through faith in Jesus Christ.**

   If you confess with your mouth that Jesus is Lord and believe in your heart that God raised him from the dead, you will be saved. For with the heart one believes and is justified, and with the mouth one confesses and is saved. For "everyone who calls on the name of the Lord will be saved." (Rom. 10:9–10, 13)

   Abram believed the Lord, and he credited it to him as righteousness. (Gen. 15:6)

   See, the enemy is puffed up; his desires are not upright—but the righteous person will live by his faithfulness. (Hab 2:4)

   ⸺⸎⸺

   Here is a prayer you can use as a guide if you would like to receive Christ:

   Lord Jesus, I need You. I believe You died on the cross for my sins. Thank You. I accept Your salvation and I receive You now as my Savior and Lord. Thank You for forgiving my sins and giving me eternal life. I give my life to You and ask You to take control of my life. Help me to live in a way that pleases You. I pray these things in Jesus' name. Amen.

NOTES

1. Gary Thomas, *Sacred Marriage: What If God Designed Marriage to Make Us Holy More than to Make Us Happy?* (Grand Rapids: Zondervan, 2000), 13.

2. See appendix 3 for all twelve steps.

3. Marian M. Schoolland, *Leading Little Ones to God: A Child's Book of Bible Teachings* (Grand Rapids: Eerdmans, 1995).

4. Beth Moore, *The Patriarchs: Encountering the God of Abraham, Isaac, and Jacob* (Nashville: LifeWay, 2005), 112.

5. Evelyn Christenson, *What Happens When Women Pray* (St. Paul: Evelyn Christenson Ministries, 2008).

6. *A League of Their Own*, Columbia Pictures, 1992.

7. Bobby Richardson, *The Bobby Richardson Story* (New York: Spire, 1965).

8. Willard F. Harley Jr., *His Needs, Her Needs: Building an Affair-Proof Marriage* (Grand Rapids: Revell, 2011).

9. See appendix 2 for other helpful books.

10. Spiros Zodhiates et al., eds., *Hebrew-Greek Key Word Study Bible: New Testament Lexical Aids* (Chatanooga: AMG Publishers, 1996), s.v. "parresia".

11. *Merriam-Webster's Collegiate Dictionary*, 11th ed. (Springfield, MA: Merriam-Webster, 2008), s.v. "confidence."

12. Spiros Zodhiates et al., eds., *Hebrew-Greek Key Word Study Bible: Old Testament Lexical Aids* (Chatanooga: AMG Publishers, 1996), 1547.

13. Nancy Leigh DeMoss, *Brokenness: The Heart God Revives* (Chicago: Moody, 2005).

14. http://www.celebraterecovery.com.

15. *Merriam-Webster's Collegiate Dictionary*, s.v. "respect."

16. For more on the subject of love and respect, read Emerson Eggerichs, *Love and Respect: The Love She Most Desires; The Respect He Desperately Needs* (Nashville: Thomas Nelson, 2004).

17. Wayne Grudem, *ESV Study Bible* (Wheaton: Crossway, 2008), 2271.

18. *Revive Our Hearts*, "The 30-Day Husband Encouragement Challenge," used with permission. You can find the full challenge, including ideas for what to do and say each day, at https://www.reviveourhearts.com/articles/30-day-husband-encouragement-challenge/.

19. Ibid.

20. See appendix 1 for more verses on marriage.

21. Taken from *Celebrate Recovery* by John Baker, copyright © 1998 by John Baker. Used by permission of Zondervan. http://www.zondervan.com.

FIERCE WOMEN

978-0-8024-0620-0

If your marriage feels like a battlefield, you need this book! Kim admits that her fierceness became a source of conflict in her marriage, but the relationship dynamic changed when she discovered her fierce strengths could be used to encourage and inspire her husband.

She knows what it's like to wrestle with the urge to control, to crave power, and to rush toward battle. In a style that makes you feel like you're having coffee with a close friend, Kim shares her story while opening the Word to reveal God's truth. This book has the tools you need to equip you to move you and your husband from adversaries to allies.

Also available as an ebook

MOODY
Publishers™

www.MoodyPublishers.com

Waiting For His Heart

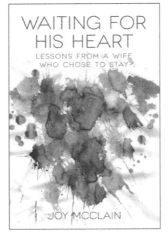

Joy intended to keep her vow to remain with her beloved Mark "no matter what."

But on her wedding day she could not have known that "no matter what" would include Mark's years-long struggle with alcohol dependency and its resulting turmoil.

Joy recounts her family's journey through these troubled times of fighting, disappointment, embarrassment, and legal separation. But she and the children never gave up on Mark as they waited for his heart to return to them.

Also available as an ebook

www.MoodyPublishers.com

LIES WOMEN BELIEVE

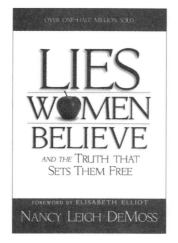

978-0-8024-7296-0

We are like Eve. We have all experienced defeats and failures, trouble and turmoil. We have all experienced a selfish heart, a shrewish spirit, anger, envy, and bitterness. And we ache to do things over, to have lives of harmony and peace. Nancy Leigh DeMoss exposes those areas of deception most commonly believed by Christian women. She sheds light on how we can be delivered from bondage and set free to walk in God's grace, forgiveness, and abundant life. The book offers the most effective weapon to encounter and overcome Satan's deceptions—God's truth.

Also available as an ebook

www.MoodyPublishers.com

Brewing rich conversations, delivering bold truth.

Pour yourself a cup of coffee and enjoy **Java with Juli**, a new podcast by host and clinical psychologist Dr. Juli Slattery. From the cozy setting of a coffee shop, Juli offers a woman's perspective on intimacy and converses with guests about the challenges of being a contemporary Christian woman.

www.moodyradio.org/javawithjuli

MOODY
Radio™